Are You Turning Into Your Dad?

Joseph Piercy

Michael O'Mara Books Limited

This paperback edition first published in 2015

First published in Great Britain in 2011 by
Michael O'Mara Books Limited
9 Lion Yard
Tremadoc Road
London SW4 7NQ

A CIP catalogue record for this book is available from the British Library.

Papers used by Michael O'Mara Books Limited are natural, recyclable products made from wood grown in sustainable forests. The manufacturing processes conform to the environmental regulations of the country of origin.

ISBN: 978-1-78243-436-8 in paperback print format
ISBN: 978-1-84317-696-1 in hardback print format
ISBN: 978-1-84317-790-6 in EPub format
ISBN: 978-1-84317-791-3 in Mobipocket format

1 2 3 4 5 6 7 8 9 10

Cover design by Dan Mogford
Designed and typeset by Design 23
Illustrations by Aubrey Smith (aubreyboxterrapin@gmail.com)

Printed and bound by CPI Group (UK) Ltd, Croydon, CR0 4YY

www.mombooks.com

Contents

INTRODUCTION

THE DAWNING REALIZATION

'Old age is the most unexpected of all the things that happen to a man.'

LEON TROTSKY

I can remember the day very clearly. It was a Friday after work and I was on my way to my parents' house when the heavens opened. I got soaked from head to toe. Stepping into the hall, I took off my dripping coat and sodden shoes and went to put them in the closet. And then it happened. I spotted them right at the back. They were an unwanted Christmas gift from a Scottish aunt a few years back. I remembered the feeling of disappointment when I'd unwrapped the box. I'd been hoping for a really cool pair of headphones but instead I got a really uncool pair of fur-lined tartan slippers. Needless to say, I'd never worn them. They were slung into the cupboard under the stairs on Boxing Day and forgotten. Until now.

Heaven Sent

My feet were wet and cold and suddenly the slippers looked unbelievably attractive. The word that sprung to mind was 'cosy'. I picked them up, turned them over in my hands and was about to put them on when my dad strolled into the hall and gave me a knowing smile. He was a dedicated fan of the softer-soled shoe, in fact, he was the only man I knew who had both a summer and a winter pair. He said one word: 'Wait'. Then he ambled over, picked up the slippers and walked into the lounge. He placed them on top of a piping hot radiator and said, 'Just give it a minute, I promise it'll be worth it.'

Worth the Wait

We waited. The minute lasted an eternity. My feet were freezing. Eventually he removed the slippers and carefully placed them in front of me. I pushed myself into them. Pure bliss. It felt like I'd stepped into a bath of lightly toasted marshmallows.

When I'd floated back down to earth I asked, 'Why didn't you tell me about this earlier?'

He was very straightforward. 'I'm sorry, son, but you just weren't ready. You wouldn't have listened, let alone appreciated what I've just done.'

I bristled, but deep down I knew he was right. I *had* been a boy – but now I was a man. 'Well is there anything else as good as this that you've been keeping to yourself?'

'Actually, there is something else I can probably share with you.'

'Such as?' I asked, expectantly.

'Have you ever sat on top of a mountain after a lengthy hike and drunk a cup of hot tea fresh from a thermos?'

No Turning Back

It was 8 March 2002 and I was thirty-two years old. That was the day I realized I was turning into my dad. And it wasn't bad. In fact, it felt really good. I was having a midlife epiphany – the opposite to a midlife crisis.

But the jump from wanting to rave all night to wanting to ramble all day can be confusing. What follows is a guidebook for fellow travellers, a lighthearted concoction of tips, quizzes and funny stories, all designed to help you understand and embrace your inner dad. So get your slippers on, ease yourself back into a comfortable armchair, take a sip of hot chocolate (no doubt from your favourite mug) and enjoy.

'The old believe everything, the middle-aged suspect everything, the young know everything.'

OSCAR WILDE

'Just remember, once you're over the hill you begin to pick up speed.'

CHARLES SCHULZ

DO YOU DRESS LIKE YOUR DAD?

THE FIRST TEST

> 'Trying on pants is one of the most humiliating things that a man can suffer that doesn't involve a woman.'
>
> LARRY DAVID

With an ever-burgeoning waistline and an ever-receding hairline one would think it'd be more important than before to be well turned out. Somehow, though, you've just let things slip these last few years. Then one day you open the wardrobe and the sinking feeling comes over you that you've started to dress like your dad. The following quiz will determine if your general attire is in desperate need of a makeover before it's too late.

1. Do you own a golf jumper, possibly in a pastel shade of yellow or purple?

☐ **Yes**   ☐ **No**

2. Is there a 'smart casual' jacket hanging in the wardrobe which you don for special occasions? You think it makes you look ten years younger but your partner vehemently protests whenever you wear it and regularly threatens to donate it to a local charity shop?

☐ **Yes**   ☐ **No**

3. Do you have a comedy loud shirt which wouldn't look out of place at a seventies-themed fancy-dress party? You secretly modelled it on the *Top Gear* presenters, although none of your family or friends have picked up on the connection.

☐ **Yes**   ☐ **No**

4. Do you still have your wedding suit, which you wear at formal occasions despite the fact it's threadbare, has immovable stains on the sleeves and is at least two decades out of fashion?

☐ **Yes**   ☐ **No**

5. Do you find entering a sports shop to buy a new pair of trainers a traumatic experience, and imagine that the shop assistants are all laughing at you behind your back?

☐ **Yes**   ☐ **No**

6. Have you developed a liking for polo shirts in plain colours?

☐ **Yes**   ☐ **No**

7. Do you insist on buying all your shoes from Hush Puppies because they're sensible and hard-wearing?

☐ **Yes**   ☐ **No**

8. Are you alarmed when you read that eighties fashions are back in vogue as you never realized they'd ever been passé?

☐ **Yes**   ☐ **No**

9. Do you buy clothes from Sunday supplement magazine 'reader offers'?

☐ Yes ☐ No

10. Do you wear socks with sandals (despite knowing it's a fashion faux pas) because you're concerned the weather might change?

☐ Yes ☐ No

Count up your number of yes and no answers. Over five yeses and you need to get your wardrobe shipshape before it's too late!

SUBSTANCE OVER STYLE

'After fifty a man discovers he does not need more than one suit.'

CLIFTON FADIMAN

'Fashion is what you adopt when you don't know who you are.'

QUENTIN CRISP

'I grow old ... I grow old ... I shall wear the bottoms of my trousers rolled.'

T. S. ELIOT

'Fashion is a form of ugliness so intolerable that we have to alter it every six months.'

OSCAR WILDE

'They should put expiration dates on clothing so we men will know when they go out of style.'

GARRY SHANDLING

'Style is knowing who you are, what you want to say and not giving a damn.'

GORE VIDAL

'My first wife divorced me because I didn't match her shoes. I was a lazy white loafer.'

KELLY MONTEITH

You Know You're Turning Into Your Dad When ...

Cast your (no doubt deteriorating) eye over the following checklist. If more than three rules apply then there's no turning back!

- The end of your tie doesn't come anywhere near the top of your trousers.

- The four-letter word for something two people can do together in bed is 'read'.

- The gleam in your eye is the sun hitting your bifocals.

- Work is a lot less fun, and fun is a lot more work.

- You can live without sex, but not without your glasses.

- You have a party and the neighbours don't even realize it.

- Your ears are hairier than your head.

- You start making maps of your wrinkles in the mirror.

DOWNTIME

TOP TEN SIGNS YOU'RE OVER THE HILL

'Middle age is having a choice between two temptations and choosing the one that'll get you home earlier.'

DAN BENNETT

Your lost weekends are a distant (and somewhat hazy) memory, and you're becoming increasingly beligerant as the years roll by. The following checklist will only serve to reconfirm your descent into middle age.

1. When you sleep, people worry you're dead.

2. Your back goes out more than you do.

3. Your best friend is dating someone half his age ... and isn't breaking any laws.

4. You split your jogging pants.

5. When your idea of a night out is sitting on the patio.

6. It takes longer to rest than it did to get tired.

7. Your address book has mostly names that start with Dr.

8. You sit in a rocking chair and can't get it going.

9. Getting 'lucky' means you found your car in the car park.

10. You forget how old you are and have to think about it.

Over the Hill

Aches and Pains

The day I realized I was over the hill was
when I went to pick up my elderly mother
from her care home to take her out for the
day and I had more trouble getting into the
car than she did! The look of pity she gave
me said it all. Talk about no going back.

GREG, FORTY-NINE

WILD WEEKENDS

'The first sign of maturity is the discovery that the volume knob also turns to the left.'

JERRY M. WRIGHT

Ah, those were the days. The lost weekends when you used to go out for a couple of drinks after work on a Friday and wake up on the floor of some random person's house sometime on Sunday afternoon. Or college days, when the weekend started on a Wednesday and finished roughly three weeks later when your overdraft had run out. These days the weekend is a short, and therefore precious, space of time between finishing work on a Friday and getting on the bus again on Monday morning, so pack them to the gunnels – just like your dad.

Are You Turning Into Your Dad?

You know you're turning into your dad if you look forward to the weekend because:

- You can go to the DIY merchants to buy a curtain rail and come back with a new set of garden furniture.

- You can go to the local farmers' market and sample the organic pies and artisan cheeses and end up spending a small fortune on homemade Thai fishcakes.

- You can go up to the allotment, do the watering and bed down your winter veg (followed by a satisfying cup of tea as you admire your hard work).

- You can clean the car – always a joy, especially if it involves going to your local automotive retailer and buying a new shammy leather and the latest all-day shine wax products.

- You've been giddy with anticipation for a Sunday morning stroll followed by a slap-up meal and a few drinks.

- You find yourself fretting about getting home in time to see the weather for the forthcoming week.

- Your idea of a heavenly weekend is a quiet night in with a DVD and a bottle of wine.

- You can listen to a radio play on Sunday morning while doing the domestic chores.

- You can wake up with a start at 7 a.m. and then have that lovely comforting feeling that you don't have to go to work.

HOBBIES
AND
INTERESTS

HEARTY PURSUITS

'Youth is the time for adventures of the body,
but age for the triumphs of the mind.'

LOGAN PEARSALL SMITH

There was a time when sitting in front of the TV with a takeaway pizza and six cans of lager seemed the perfect way to spend your leisure hours. But on the approach to middle age you soon realize life is quickly passing you by, so it's therefore time to do something more constructive instead.

Pottering Around in the Garden

A common sign that you're turning into your dad is to develop an interest in gardening. Never having had the slightest of leanings towards being in any way 'green-fingered', suddenly the garden offers an escape from domestic toil and workplace troubles. Spouses or partners will find it hard to criticize you for devoting time and a little energy to the horticultural arts. Be it mowing the lawn, trimming the hedges or growing your own fruit and vegetables, a few precious hours each week of solitary peace will set you firmly on the path of righteousness. Should you happen to make a bit of a dog's dinner of the garden in the process, you can always fall back on Janet Kilburn Phillips' mantra that 'there are no gardening mistakes, only experiments'.

'The best way to garden is to put on a wide-brimmed straw hat and some old clothes. And with a hoe in one hand and a cold beer in the other, tell someone else where to dig.'

TEXAS BIX BENDER

'A society grows great when old men plant trees whose shade they know they shall never sit in.'

ANCIENT GREEK PROVERB

'Like a big mountain, a small garden
stimulates, restores and delights us, just
as it poses challenges, promotes mastery,
provides exercise and relieves monotony.'
WINIFRED GALLAGHER, *THE POWER OF PLACE*

Researching Your Family History

Perhaps you always considered yourself the black
sheep of the family? Maybe you harboured thoughts of
greatness in your youth? The onset of middle age has
brought with it the realization that all of those dreams
have long since passed, and so it's time now to turn
to former glories by researching your family history.
Discovering that a distant relative may have fought
at the Battle of Waterloo or an ancient ancestor was
a footman to the Earl of Queensbury provides some
small comfort against that nagging feeling that your life
has been fairly unfulfilled. There's also much scope for
poetic licence with the flimsiest morsels of information
blown out of all proportion as you trawl through public
record libraries and online genealogy websites in your
quest to prove that at some point in the past a member
of your family did something significant.

Making Sense . . .

I got a bit worried when my dad suddenly started researching the family history. I thought, *what if he uncovers some unpleasant skeletons, like finding out our family were involved in the slave trade, or were Nazi collaborators?* In the end I realized he was probably just trying to make sense of it all, and no doubt I'll get to that point soon too.

JIM, THIRTY-SEVEN

'If you cannot get rid of the family skeleton, you may as well make it dance.'

GEORGE BERNARD SHAW

'There is no king who has not had a slave among his ancestors, and no slave who has not had a king among his.'

HELEN KELLER

37

Visiting Old Relics

Many a childhood family holiday was blighted by visits to old relics, like churches and castles. The nearest you ever got to a theme park was the rickety old rollercoaster on the seafront for which the term 'health and safety' was created. However, the despair you felt as a child being dragged around country houses, despondently ticking off boxes in *I-Spy* books, was actually great preparation for later life. You too can now subject your family to long and fretful car rides in search of places of dubious interest and educational value. It's a great way of reliving all those mundane public holidays of your youth.

Essential Rules for the Relic Dweller:

- On arrival, greet the austere and curmudgeonly car park attendant with forced jollity and a suitably cringeworthy term of address, such as 'Morning, chieftain!'

- Adopt the appropriate stance when reading information plaques: stand with feet evenly spaced and the torso bent forward at an angle of roughly thirty degrees, both hands should be clasped behind the back and an expression of slightly quizzical earnestness worn.

- Maintain a sense of boundless enthusiasm for any of the admittedly mediocre entertainment on offer, especially if it involves out-of-work actors re-enacting historical battles. Exuberant audience participation is also essential, so heckle to your heart's content (much to the horror of any teenage children you may have in tow).

'After a man passes sixty, his mischief is mainly in his head.'

WASHINGTON IRVING

A Magical Mystery Tour

My dad would never tell us where he was taking us to on family outings. A big fan of The Beatles in his youth, he would claim that we were on 'a magical mystery tour'. Invariably we would roll up at some country house and Dad would pretend we'd happened upon it by mistake and say, 'Wow, let's go and explore.' It was only years later that I realized this was a ploy to 'sell' visiting somewhere he wanted to visit, but knew we would find boring, by pretending it was a random and spontaneous adventure. Genius tactic, or so I thought, until I tried it with my own daughter, who simply gave me a withering look and said, 'Just tell me where we're going.' Perhaps children aren't as gullible these days.

JAMES, FORTY-TWO

Not Only Doing but Actually Enjoying DIY

There was a time in the not too distant past when your dad could be relied upon to pop round and do a couple of nagging DIY jobs you'd been steadfastly avoiding. You were atrocious at putting together flat-pack furniture, with every attempt resulting in rickety dining chairs and wonky bookshelves, and your dad's methodical approach to such jobs enraged you to the point of apoplexy. Why do a job properly if you can do it slapdash and still make the pub in time for kick-off?

And then one day the penny drops and you start actually reading the instructions and laying out and counting all the parts in the flatpack. A toolbox mysteriously appears in the shed, trips to the DIY shop no longer fill you with intolerable loathing and you suddenly know exactly which aisle stocks plug sockets. Most startling of all, you actually enjoy those fiddly little jobs that used to leave you feeling inadequate, and you now take pride in your workmanship and knowledge of a job well done.

* * *

In an episode of the hit US television sitcom *Home Improvement*, accident-prone handyman Tim Taylor (Tim Allen) tries to deflect criticism from his son Brad concerning his ineptitude around the house:

Tim: 'Kids turn into their parents, I don't know what it is. One day you're going to turn into me.'

Brad: 'Boy, I'm gonna need a lot of medical insurance.'

Do It Yourself?

The first flat I bought was an absolute hole, and added to that I didn't have a penny to my name so was forced to employ my very negligible DIY skills to try and make it in some way habitable. But blunt saws and cack-handed blokes don't mix! After I nearly sliced off the index finger on my left hand I realized it was time to get in some help. Luckily my dad was very handy and came to the rescue. Watching him take such pride in his work inspired me to calm down and take my time with my DIY. Now I love nothing more than spending my weekend crafting my latest project – much to my wife's annoyance!

BILL, FORTY-ONE

Chewing the Fat Over the Garden Fence With the Neighbours

You always used to adopt an attitude towards your neighbours akin to classic Victorian attitudes to children: they should be rarely seen and certainly not heard. The only time you'd ever had any dealings with them was when they came round to complain you were playing your music too loud, or that you'd taken their prized parking space.

Recently, however, you've found yourself leaning on the garden wall of a Sunday morning making small talk about the weather or your local sports team's chances in the upcoming Cup game. Before you know it you're putting a Christmas card through their door and inviting them round for New Year's drinks, sampling their homebrewed hooch, swapping spare keys and feeding their pets when they go on holiday.

> 'For age is opportunity no less
> Than youth itself, though in another dress,
> And as the evening twilight fades away,
> The sky is filled with stars invisible by day.'
>
> HENRY WADSWORTH LONGFELLOW,
> 'MORITURI SALUTAMUS', 1875

Drinking Ale

The days and nights of supping continental lagers have long since passed – these days you find they're much too 'gassy' and 'repeat on you' at inopportune moments. And the stronger varieties have fearsome hangover potential and give you migraines. So now is the time to follow Dad in his passion for beer and local microbreweries.

> 'Words are not as satisfactory as we should like them to be, but, like our neighbours, we have got to live with them and must make the best and not the worst of them.'
>
> SAMUEL BUTLER

Just Checking

Whenever my grandfather received a glass of beer he had this habit of holding it up to the light to check the clarity of the drink. In recent years I've noticed my father doing the same thing. Last week I was in a pub with my wife and she went to the bar and returned with a pint. Without thinking, I picked up the glass and held it up to the light. 'What are you looking for?' she asked. 'You know what?' I replied, 'I haven't the faintest idea.'

SIMON, FORTY-ONE

Reading the Sunday Papers

Sunday mornings during your twenties used to either pass you by completely or were spent in a state of such physical disrepair you could barely see straight, let alone read. But hark back even further to the Sunday mornings of your childhood when you accompanied your dad down to the newsagent's for a pint of milk and the Sunday paper. This arcane ritual is worth persisting with now that you wake up on a weekend at roughly the time you used to be going to bed. A quick stroll to take in the air and stretch your legs, and then back home to cook breakfast and peruse the week's news at your leisure: it's what Sundays were meant for all along.

Listening to Spoken Radio

The latest dance music anthems haven't filled your ears since your clubbing days two decades ago and you find most music radio stations aggravate your tinnitus. So, time to turn to the serene comforts of spoken radio. You're much more likely these days to be more au fait with the latest happenings in the world's current affairs than the latest happening bands.

Don't Shout at the Radio

The *Today* programme was on the radio every morning at the behest of my dad. My older sister used to complain as all her friends listened to the Radio One *Breakfast Show* with Mike Read. My dad would get really annoyed with the politicians they interviewed on the *Today* programme and would shout at the wireless. My mum would say, 'Turn it off if it's upsetting you.' Lately I've found myself hollering abuse at the radio on more than one occasion, much to the irritation of my partner.

STEVE, THIRTY-SEVEN

Joining Your Local Community Action Group

The notion that you would ever take up the role of a high-minded local do-gooder would have seemed absurd before you entered parenthood. Perhaps it's the natural instinct to protect your offspring from harm. Perhaps, more depressingly, it may also be that as your life has become less interesting, your interest in the lives of other people has increased.

Nobody in their right mind likes to be thought of as a curtain-twitching busybody, so one way of satisfying your curiosity about the goings-on in your local area could be to join a local residents' association. The monthly meetings will provide opportunities aplenty to have a good old moan about various things that have been getting you down, such as dog mess in the local parks, late-night noise from nearby pubs or the groups of hoodies congregating at the end of your road. And you might even get some free tea and biscuits too!

'Grow old along with me!
The best is yet to be.
The last of life, for which the first was made.'
ROBERT BROWNING, 'RABBI BEN EZRA'

THE SPORTING GENTLEMAN

'Playing golf is like going to a strip joint: after eighteen holes you are tired and most of your balls are missing.'

TIM ALLEN

Sports, to paraphrase former Liverpool FC manager Bill Shankly, used to be more important than a matter of life and death – your team losing to their fiercest rivals would send you spiralling into days of gloomy depression. Suddenly the day arrives when you realize that you've invested far too much emotional energy into something that you have about as much control over as the weather.

It's at this point that those rose-tinted spectacles come out again and you start to hark back to the heroes of your youth and indulge largely bogus notions of the Corinthian Spirit. You begin to find yourself saying things like, 'The problem with football is there's too much money in it,' or, 'Rugby's not been the same since they turned professional.' These were, of course, the exact same arguments your dad used to reel out when you were young, although advancements in political correctness forbid the use of the phrase 'over-paid poofters'.

It's Not the Winning That Matters, It's the Taking Part

Your list of sporting achievements is pretty negligible, yet somehow the further they recede into the past, the larger they become when viewed through the prism of time. Take, for example, the match-saving thirteen not out you scored for the school second eleven, or the headed equalizer for the Cubs in an under-twelves seven-a-side tournament – memories of these minor moments of triumph aren't enough to satisfy your competitive instincts and you still feel you've plenty to offer the world of sporting endeavour. The prospect of playing five-a-side football fills you with terror so, after taking stock of your general levels of ill health, below are some alternatives to delude yourself that you've still got it where it matters.

'Long ago when men cursed and beat the ground with sticks it was called witchcraft. Today it's called golf.'

ANON

Just Not Cricket?

So what of the Corinthian Spirit and its virtues of fair play and gentlemanliness? Well, despite your best intentions, these rules are thrown quickly out of the window when your own pub cricket team gets together for a match. You roll up each spring for the weekly net practice, which consists of one hour of tossing down a few balls at a gentle pace, followed by three hours in the nearest pub discussing the season ahead. So far so Corinthian – after all, you're doing it for the love of the game, to get some exercise and not at all using it as an excuse to spend two Sundays a month drinking with your friends.

Invariably there's a grudge match once a season against a rival pub with whom there was some 'bad blood' a few years ago. All notion of 'it's not the winning that matters, it's the taking part' is tossed aside as you pressgang a couple of 'chaps' from work into coming and playing for you as ringers against the enemy. Unfortunately the opposition has had exactly the same idea, only its ringers are considerably better than yours. To make matters worse you've roped your dad in as umpire and, ever the stickler for rules, he promptly gives you out leg before wicket. The sight of you having a stand-up row with your dad in the middle of the pitch is just about as far from the Corinthian Spirit as you can possibly get.

'Golf is a day spent in a round of strenuous idleness.'

WILLIAM WORDSWORTH

Golf – a Good Walk Spoiled

It's a fiendishly difficult game to play, and it's safe to say that if you're coming to golf late in life then you're never going to master it. What golf does provide, though, amid many hours of frustration, are possibilities to make a lot out of very little. There was that time you 'chipped in' from the bunker or holed a thirty-foot putt for par – precious moments that owe more to luck than talent.

Another appealing aspect of taking up golf is the opportunity to accessorize. The club shop is a treasure trove of largely useless gadgets you can invest in which will have little effect on your ability to play the game. And then there's the nineteenth hole where you can prop up the bar and relive your round over a pint or three. On the downside, developing an interest in golf can be misconstrued by relatives and friends as actually being interested *in* golf and, as a result, every Christmas someone will buy you some mind-numbingly unfunny book of golfing wit and wisdom.

It's All in the Outfit

My dad decided quite inexplicably to take up golf at the grand old age of fifty-two. He struggled to master the notoriously difficult game so chose instead to focus on the all-important accessories. From a flat cap and pastel jumper, right the way down to a pair of argyle socks – he thought he looked the business. My brother and I would crease ourselves laughing when we saw him come down the stairs in all his regalia. Of course I'm now laughing on the other side of my face as I've just paid out an extortionate amount for some introductory golf lessons, and it's inevitable I'll receive at least one golfing accessory this Christmas.

MICHAEL, FORTY-SIX

'The place of the father in the modern suburban family is a very small one, particularly if he plays golf.'

BERTRAND RUSSELL

'The golf course is the only place I can go dressed like a pimp and fit in perfectly. Anywhere else – lime-green pants and alligator shoes – I got a cop on my ass.'

SAMUEL L. JACKSON

'The meek will inherit the earth but they won't make the green in two.'

LEE TREVINO

Crown Green Bowls

A much less rigorous pursuit, or at least requiring less trudging around than golf, is crown green bowls. A gentle sport, bowls has a regal-like serenity attached to it on account of Sir Francis Drake's refusal to contemplate the oncoming Spanish Armada until he'd finished his game. Long idle afternoons await the fledgling bowls enthusiast, and the fact that it's an easy game to learn means that even the most ill co-ordinated of people can master the basics.

EVERYDAY LIFE

HOME COMFORTS

'Middle age is when your age starts to show around your middle.'

BOB HOPE

No middle-aged man who's starting to resemble his dad would be without at least three of the following top five beloved home comforts:

1. Indulging the *Special* Armchair

Usually a threadbare affair acquired either from a car boot sale (having a 'nose' for a bargain that's very much in the eye of the beholder is a skill that comes with advancing years) or from the house clearance of a deceased relative – the special armchair is to be afforded particular affection. The chair should be as conspicuous as possible and belligerently refuse to fit in with any other furniture in the house. Moreover, it's universally despised by partners, with barely a weekend passing without a row about when the mite-ridden monstrosity is going to be taken to the nearest dump. It's important to remain implacable in the face of this relationship rancour and stick firmly to your guns. Develop a belief that the special armchair has potential antique value and that 'they don't make 'em like this anymore'. Wave goodbye to any notion of common sense and pay an extortionate amount of money to have it re-upholstered in a sub-William Morris flocked floral pattern. Convince yourself that you and only you (and occasionally the cat) are allowed to sit on it – this is a fairly easy rule to enforce as the cast-iron springs have inevitably rusted beyond repair and, in truth, the chair wouldn't be out of place in a medieval torture chamber. Eventually, of course, the strain of holding out against a barrage of constant moans and gripes, not to mention the nagging feeling that the special armchair is doing your back complaint (see Health and Ailments, page 78), will force a partial compromise and the armchair can be retired to the garden shed (see over).

2. Collecting Pointless Kitchen Accessories

A new-found interest in the culinary arts (inspired by a devotion to *Masterchef* and deviant fantasies about Nigella Lawson) invariably leads to the purchase of thoroughly unnecessary kitchen accessories. These can take the form of a pasta machine or fondue set, but they're likely to only ever be used on a handful of occasions before being consigned to the back of a cupboard. A better option is to purchase something that can be used to cook your signature dish, such as an omelette pan.

3. Maintaining a Slavish Devotion to Outmoded Technological Gadgets

Any attempt to keep abreast of new technology has long since been abandoned, particularly as sixteen-bit megapixel sounds like a citation on the shipping forecast. Far better to keep your trusty old Nokia and steadfastly refuse to upgrade. The numbers have rubbed off the keypad and the battery cells are on their last legs but 'it does a job'. The same could also be said of the cranky old, virus-ridden PC that crackles and takes half a day to boot up – after all, you can always get a friend of a friend's brother who drinks down your local to come round and clean it up for you (saving on the embarrassment of taking it

into a shop, where your ignorance is going to be well and truly exposed).

4. Spending Long Hours in the Shed

It's a well-acknowledged fact that dads love sheds. It's both a haven of peace and a treasure trove in which to hoard all manner of junk that you just can't bear to throw away. Time spent in the shed is time well served, and, moreover, the shed can become the focal point for all manner of pet projects and passing fads, from home brewing to remote-controlled aircraft building.

One Man and His Shed

My dad spent hours and hours in the shed supposedly fixing things. My brother and I were banned from going in there, supposedly because there were dangerous tools lying around. If he ever caught us poking about in his shed he'd go bananas. After he died we found a stack of old seventies soft-porn magazines in a box under the workbench. We didn't have the heart to tell Mum, but I expect she probably knew – she just didn't want them in the house.

MARK, FORTY-TWO

5. Sporting a Dressing Gown and Slippers

Few items of clothing will give you as much pleasure as the dressing gown. The dressing gown first became popular amongst the British and Dutch aristocracy in the mid-seventeenth century, not as bed wear but as an informal *banyan* or 'house coat'. The *banyan* was a loose kimono-style dress with flared sleeves, usually made from Indian or Chinese silk, and was worn by men of culture and intellect – loose, comfortable attire for when one was in the library attending to 'one's books' (the modern-day equivalent would be whilst on the loo reading the paper).

There are a number of very important rules that should be observed when sporting a dressing gown:

The Rules

1. The gown must come down to the knee and include a belt or tie.

2. It should be made from thick material or be quilted – you're going to be wearing it outside when visiting the shed or sneaking out the back for a crafty cigarette.

3. It should always be worn accompanied by another dear friend: a pair of slippers. A dressing gown without slippers is like Benson without Hedges – it doesn't make sense.

4. Pockets are a must for hiding things that would usually be filed under For Your Eyes Only, such as tobacco, lighters, Rizla, even mobile phone bills.

5. Do not wash your dressing gown more than once a year – every stain and cigarette burn tells a story.

Famous Dressing Gowns of the Past ...

The thinking man's dress of choice:

- The physicist Sir Isaac Newton did much of his thinking while swanning around his house and garden in his dressing gown.

- Throughout Douglas Adams' book *The Hitchhiker's Guide to the Galaxy* the hero, Arthur Dent, wears a dressing gown.

- Oscar Wilde once said, 'One should either be a work of art, or wear a work of art.' His work of art was his customary smoking jacket, which he no doubt wore when writing his latest masterpiece.

- Sherlock Holmes' favourite indoor attire was a dressing gown.

'Loose dresses contribute to the easy and vigorous exercise of the faculties of the mind. This remark is so obvious, and so generally known, that we find studious men are always painted in gowns when they are seated in their libraries.'

BENJAMIN RUSH

MANNERISMS AND GESTURES

'Old age: first you forget names, then you forget faces, then you forget to pull your zipper up, then you forget to pull your zipper down.'

LEO ROSENBERG

It's inevitable really – we learn through imitation at a young age, and so it's heartwarming to know this continues in later life as we unintentionally start to copy the little gestures and mannerisms our parents used.

Harrumphing

The classic 'harrumph' is a cross between a growl and a sigh and has many purposes: it's most commonly used when sitting down on or standing up from the sofa or armchair; a weary exhalation that signifies either relief at having just completed some dull domestic chore or mild irritation at the prospect of attempting one. As Bill Crosby, harrumphing as he gets up from the sofa, put it, 'What was that noise? That was my father's noise.'

Adopting the Benign Smile

A useful weapon to have in your mannerisms and gestures armoury, the benign smile is used when listening to a relative or friend recounting details of their recent holiday (using phrases like 'you would have loved this little restaurant we found'). The benign smile should be punctuated with a rueful nod so as to assure the person telling the story that you're listening to them and not thinking about Jenny Agutter in the film of *The Railway Children*, or the menu at your favourite restaurant.

Staring into the Middle Distance

So you've got out of the armchair and harrumphed. Now it's time to go to another room in the house and, on arrival, realize you've momentarily forgotten what you were about to do. Go to the window and look outside – there'll be something you can stare at in the middle distance for a few moments while you wait for your brain to catch up: a magpie to salute in a tree in the garden or some building work going on in the house across the road. These vacant moments are precious and to be savoured in the grind of everyday life.

> 'Did you ever walk into a room and forget why you walked in? I think that's how dogs spend their lives.'
>
> SUE MURPHY

Humming Softly to Yourself

It's unclear when you started humming. Perhaps you've always done it; perhaps your dad has always been a hummer too. However, you suddenly realize that you aren't humming any tune in particular. Instead you're emitting a series of random notes in a staccato sequence that bear a resemblance to fragments of the *William Tell Overture* played backwards. If you were to record all of these abstract hums from your internal orchestra they would probably make quite an agreeable avant-garde symphony in B minor.

'As you get older three things happen: the first is your memory goes, and I can't remember what the other two are.'

SIR NORMAN WISDOM

The Pregnant Pause

Inserting a pregnant pause into a conversation gives the impression that what you're about to say has considerable gravitas; something insightful and worth listening to. Or at least that's what you hope people will think. You certainly wouldn't want them to think you've forgotten the point of what you were saying ...

Looking for one's pipe, then realizing it's in one's mouth, or for one's specs, pushed back on top of one's head – that can happen to anyone. But again and again, looking up foreign words in bilingual dictionaries, English/French, English/German, in the wrong half of the book ... What is distinctly worse, I tell myself 'dictionary', I must look up some word in the dictionary, to check on spelling or pronunciation. When I arrive at the word, I gaze at it uncomprehendingly: it is 'dictionary'.

D.J. ENRIGHT, *PLAY RESUMED: A JOURNAL*

Dancing Very Badly

Slightly more energetic, but no less important, the dad dance is a strange phenomenon. You consider yourself to have been something of a mover in your youth, but these days the shapes you throw are more Michael Bolton than Michael Jackson. It starts off with a slow tap of the right foot, then your arms start twitching and your head bobs quickly from side to side. Before you know it all three are moving together with no regard to the rhythm of the music, and your kids are standing from the sidelines laughing their heads off. Welcome to the world of dad dancing.

Smooth Moves

I always thought it was a cliché that once you pass the age of thirty-five you should avoid the dance floor unless you want to look like a dad dancing at a wedding. I was round at my parents' the other day and they got out the video of my younger sister's wedding a few months back. To my horror I caught sight of myself jiving enthusiastically to an old Donna Summer disco belter along with my father. It wasn't that I was dancing 'like a dad' – I was dancing exactly like my dad.

TIM, THIRTY-EIGHT

WISE WORDS

You secretly used to derive great comfort from your dad's classic phrases and now find yourself using the very same lines in an attempt to soothe your own brood. Faster than you can say, 'What an almighty racket', or, 'This place looks like a bomb's hit it', your everyday vocabulary has become littered with your dad's favourite sayings.

Dad Talk

Let There Be Light!

On entering the house to find all of the lights on my dad would always stomp around switching them off, muttering, 'This isn't Blackpool bloody Illuminations you know!' I haven't yet let on to him that I too now use that phrase when my fifteen-year-old leaves all the house lights on!

JASON, FORTY-NINE

I Knows 'Em . . .

When serving up home-grown vegetables
from his allotment, Dad would always brim
with pride and say, 'I knows 'em, I grows
'em.' But when I recently pulled my perfectly
home-grown potatoes out from the ground
and proclaimed the very same, my wife's
bewildered look said it all.

CHRIS, FORTY-TWO

Cliché? Moi?

My dad had a selection of stock phrases that
he'd roll out for different situations. They
became his own family clichés and he used
them so often we became completely used
to them. The weird thing is I've noticed myself
doing it more and more, and even using some
of Dad's favourite sayings myself.

DOMINIC, FIFTY-ONE

Are We There Yet?

In response to the inevitable whinging during long car journeys my father had a series of sayings. For example, if either myself or one of my siblings asked, 'Are we there yet?' my father would reply, 'We'll be there when we arrive.' It never occurred to me that this was stating the blaringly obvious!

JAN, TWENTY-NINE

Rebel Without a Cause

In a well-meaning but fruitless attempt to sanction the behaviour of my rebellious older sister, Dad would call an impromptu family meeting over dinner and start off by saying, 'There are going to be a few changes round here from now on.' This became quite comforting after a while as it actually meant that things were pretty much going to stay exactly the same.

MIKE, FORTY-FIVE

The Magic Word

My father was obsessive about manners and particularly saying 'please' and 'thank you'. If you asked somebody to pass the salt at the table and didn't say 'please' he'd immediately bark, 'Say the magic word.' I tried this recently with my eight-year-old daughter when she asked for a drink. 'What's the magic word?' I asked as sternly as I could. 'Abracadabra,' she replied with a shrug.

DAN, THIRTY-NINE

'Parents are the bones on which children sharpen their teeth.'

PETER USTINOV

Salty Seadog

My dad had a weird phrase for most occasions. One that always stuck with me was, whenever we pulled up somewhere in the car, he'd shout, 'All ashore that's going ashore! Pick up your parrots and monkeys!' like he was some sort of pirate. I've no idea where he got it from, but it use to embarrass the hell out of me if I had a mate from school in the car at the time … Doesn't stop me saying it now, though!

ALISTAIR, FIFTY-TWO

Hairy Chest

Whenever my father gave you a drink or served a meal he'd always say, 'That'll put hairs on your chest!' Was it any wonder I couldn't keep a girlfriend for long? Luckily my wife thought he was sweet. But there were times I could have crowned my old man. Now, of course, I can't wait for my boy to bring a girl home!

ROGER, FORTY-THREE

Sound Advice

My dad was a bit of a sage and if I was worrying unnecessarily about something he'd always crack out the same line: 'If you think you can, or you think you can't, you probably will.' A bit of a tongue-twister, which often took me a while to decipher, but now I'm a bit older I realize how right he was. All those years battling against his advice were a bit fruitless. And I now even use the phrase on my own kids!

ANDREW, FORTY-ONE

WHEN THE GOING GETS TOUGH

HEALTH AND AILMENTS

'After thirty, a body has a mind of its own.'

BETTE MIDLER

You know you're turning into your dad when the list of mundane but nonetheless debilitating ailments from which you suffer starts to grow year by year.

Here are a few that you may recognize, and a few which will require immediate treatment (the sooner the better).

Tennis Elbow

The classic 'sports injury' (although regular tennis and squash players make up a small proportion of sufferers) is a painful form of rheumatism affecting the elbow bone. Tennis elbow has its uses, though, and often tends to come on suddenly when there's any heavy lifting or carrying to be done.

'I went to see the doctor and he said, "You've got hypochondria." I said, "Not that as well!"'

TIM VINE

Trapped Nerves

You know you're in decline when you wake up one morning and find that you've ricked your neck or pulled your shoulder in your sleep. The most depressing aspects of trapping a nerve in this way are that you've no idea how you did it and there's no real cure. Friends and family treat your complaint with considerable suspicion, and attempts to relieve the pain through the purchase of numerous 'deep heat' products are fruitless and expensive.

> 'It's no longer a question of staying healthy. It's just a question of finding a sickness you like.'
>
> JACKIE MASON

Sciatica

Another mystery ailment that often appears completely out of the blue. One day you're flying down a zip wire runway with the kids at your local adventure playground, the next you can barely get out of bed.

> 'Be careful about reading health books. You may die of a misprint.'
>
> MARK TWAIN

Gout

There's little comfort to be gleaned from suffering 'the disease of kings', as it's known. This painful form of inflammatory arthritis can often be attributed to dietary concerns, with the usual suspects such as coffee, dairy products (especially rich cheeses), red wine, seafood and red meat are the prime suspects – basically anything worth eating in the world.

'Like everybody else, when I don't know what else to do, I seem to go in for catching colds.'

GEORGE JEAN NATHAN

Haemorrhoids

The dreaded piles that your grandmother warned you about. To begin with you think it's just a by-product of the chicken madras and several pints you consumed the night before. Several days later the increasing discomfort is starting to play havoc with your natural tendencies towards hypochondria. The next thing you know you're suffering the indignity of a trip to the GP for an inspection.

I THINK I MIGHT BE COMING DOWN WITH SOMETHING . . .

'I'm so psychosomatic, it makes me feel sick just thinking about it.'

LARRY DAVID

'Hypochondria is Greek for "men".'

KATHY LETTE

'Every man who feels well is just a sick man neglecting himself.'

ROBERT ORBEN

'If a man thinks about his physical or moral state he usually discovers that he is ill.'

JOHANN WOLFGANG VON GOETHE

'We drink one another's health and spoil our own.'

JEROME K. JEROME

'I hate waiting rooms. Because it's called the waiting room there's no chance of not waiting. It's built, designed and intended for waiting. Why would they see you right away when they've got this room all set up.'

JERRY SEINFELD

'People who are always taking care of their health are like misers who are hoarding a treasure which they have never spirit enough to enjoy.'

LAURENCE STERNE

'My memory is going. I brush my teeth and ten minutes later I go back and have to feel the toothbrush. Is it wet? Did I just brush them?'

TERRY GILLIAM

'The trouble with always trying to preserve the health of the body is that it is so difficult to do without destroying the health of the mind.'

G.K. CHESTERTON

STARTING TO LOSE THE PLOT?

'Men, like peaches and pears, grow sweet a little while before they begin to decay.'

OLIVER WENDELL HOLMES, SR

It's Monday morning and you're late for work. The kids are still eating their breakfast and school is meant to start in ten minutes. As you scramble to get everyone out of the door you realize you've misplaced your car keys. You're sure you left them by the front door when you came in yesterday. Retracing your footsteps from the night before, you finally find the keys down the back of the sofa, only to get into the car and realize you've forgotten where it is you're supposed to be going. Ever feel like you're starting to lose the plot?

'Middle age is when you still believe you'll feel better in the morning.'

BOB HOPE

Get Your Hair Filled

I got home from work last Friday and
suddenly remembered I had a haircut
appointment. I checked the calendar and
found the appointment card pinned to
the day's date. I hurriedly grabbed my
coat and rushed out, mindful that I was
running late. On arrival at the hairdresser
the receptionist could find no reference of
my booking. I explained that I'd pinned the
card to the date on the calendar and that
it must be an oversight on their part. The
receptionist booked me for the following day
and apologized profusely. When I got home
I double-checked and sure enough I had
had an appointment at four forty-five p.m.
Unfortunately, the appointment card was for
the dentist, not the hairdresser.

WILLIAM, FORTY-SEVEN

Technologically Challenged

I recently purchased a new car stereo radio with a CD player on eBay. I was particularly pleased with my purchase as I'd been bidding for it for a week and had won the auction at what I considered to be a bargain price. The seller, however, was somewhat tardy with sending my prize through and I started to get a bit twitchy that I'd been ripped off. After a few terse emails the car stereo finally arrived without its box and not quite in the pristine condition I'd anticipated. In fact, it was just a radio and not a CD player at all. I was in the process of sending in a complaint to eBay when my teenage son came into the room and started inspecting the machine. 'Cool CD player,' he said, flipping open a hitherto concealed flap on the front of the stereo.

MIKE, FORTY-EIGHT

'The first forty years of life give us the text: the next thirty supply the commentary.'

ARTHUR SCHOPENHAUER

Cat Tales

My neighbour recently asked me if I minded feeding her cat while she went away. 'You only have to go in once a day and put the food out,' she said. 'The cat's very shy and won't come out until you've gone.' So I duly did as she asked but found the cat to be very friendly. It'd be waiting for me by the back door when I arrived and would curl around my legs as I dished out its dinner. We definitely struck up a great bond. When my neighbour returned I gushed about her lovely ginger tom but she looked at me rather oddly and said, 'My cat's a tabby.' I mumbled something inaudible, took the gift she'd bought me as a thank you and backed away. Clearly I'd spent the previous two weeks feeding the wrong animal. God knows what state her cat was in after a fortnight of foraging for scraps.

GRAHAM, THIRTY-THREE

Tour of Duty

I went to a classical music concert at our local church (which is a whole other story) and during the half-time booze interval I nipped out for a fag. Some of the young musicians involved in the concert – and we're talking quite accomplished Royal School of Music types here – were skulking outside, sharing a joint. But my arrival at the scene had the same impact as the deputy head doing a tour of duty round the bike sheds during the dinner hour: they quickly scarpered. I suppose there was a time when they'd have offered me a 'hit'…

NEIL, FORTY-SIX

Wrong Decade

I had back surgery recently and while talking to my (very pretty) physiotherapist, I discovered we had a lot in common: we were both born in Chicago and had grown up in the same area. We got talking about schools and I mentioned I'd been at CU Boulder in 1977. It turned out she went to CU too, so perhaps we'd met before. But of course she was there in 1999. Oops! I really wasn't thinking. I'm really bad at judging age sometimes.

JEFF, FIFTY-FOUR

An American Dad Discusses the Changes That Have Occurred Since the Age of Thirty-Five

I've heard that the midlife crisis is very difficult, but I never expected it to hit me. But hit me it has and, boy, has it been quite an adjustment.

It didn't just happen overnight, though – it really snuck up on me. My brain didn't process the fact that I was hitting middle age until one day I looked down and realized that my six-pack had morphed into a seven, and I'd suddenly started to look a lot like my dad.

Here's a quick rundown of all the changes I've undergone since the age of thirty-five:

- I can't sit down for longer than five minutes at a time because if I do I hurt in places I didn't even know existed. I have to soak in the bathtub for a good hour after any physical exertion. Even then, I'm still in pain.

- A total failure to understand what the word 'cool' actually means. When I was growing up, if you said something was 'cool' it meant that it was a good thing. But now if you say something is 'cool' you're definitely implying that you're a huge fan of joss sticks and Def Leppard. If you add a peace sign, then you suddenly become a dated dad that cannot possibly see past 1980.

- My joints are so noisy I sound like a one-man band using nothing but my bones for instruments.

- I've become VERY hairy, sprouting some of the longest hairs you've ever seen. I'm getting quite bored of plucking my extra long nose hairs.

- I've suddenly developed a mild case of narcolepsy and can't seem to get through the afternoon without a nap. The other day, for instance, I fell asleep in the middle of a Chicago Bears NFL Championship game.

- I keep my wife awake every night with the sound of my snoring. It's so loud, she says it sounds like the arrival of a freight train.

- I'm over-emotional, especially when it comes to the small things – a kitten, a giant hot dog at half-time. The all-time game breaker though is the end of *The Wizard of Oz* when the Tin Man says, 'Now I know I have a heart because I can feel it breaking.'

RANDY, FORTY-TWO

OCD Quiz

'Age seldom arrives smoothly or quickly. It's more often a succession of jerks.'

JEAN RHYS

One awful psychological tick that stalks you through the small hours of the day is the thought that you've somehow genetically inherited the same obsessive-compulsive disorders as your dad. The following quiz will either leave you feeling slightly unnerved but ultimately relieved, or wailing in despair.

1. Have you started to fret about whether members of your family or staying guests leave the bathroom light on overnight?

☐ **Yes**   ☐ **No**

2. After leaving the house, do you return to double-check you've deadlocked the door even though you can remember quite vividly doing so?

☐ **Yes**   ☐ **No**

3. Do your anxiety levels go through the roof when a household appliance breaks down?

☐ **Yes**   ☐ **No**

4. Do you find yourself following the same rituals before going to bed? (E.g. hot drink, check the back door is locked, feed the cat, double-check the back door is locked, double-check you've fed the cat.)

☐ **Yes**   ☐ **No**

5. Have you ever found yourself counting down the days until the council come round and pick up your recycling?

☐ Yes   ☐ No

6. Have you found yourself fearful of throwing out old, threadbare and largely unfashionable items of clothing in the mistaken belief that they may come in useful one day (or may even come back into fashion!)?

☐ Yes   ☐ No

7. Do you fixate on keeping the bathroom clean due to a morbid fascination with the spread of germs?

☐ Yes   ☐ No

8. Have you found yourself meticulously checking your weekly shopping receipts at the checkout in your local supermarket to make sure the checkout operator has taken off the discounts due for multi-buy offers?

☐ Yes ☐ No

9. Do you sniff the milk and other perishable food products every time you open the fridge?

☐ Yes ☐ No

10. Do you obsess about losing your wallet, keys and mobile phone, and check your pockets at least once every ten minutes (known as the 'pocket patting' dance) to check they're still there, and/or keep them on your person at all times?

☐ Yes ☐ No

Results

Mostly 'yes':

OK, you probably don't have OCD and there's largely nothing wrong with having any of the above habits and rituals as long as they're not causing you to become over-anxious, to lose sleep or become depressed. The chances are that you've got to the point in your life where losing your keys, needlessly wasting money and living in squalor no longer holds any 'bohemian' appeal and you've merely started to smarten up your act a bit. Your dad, in this respect, is a valuable role model.

Mostly 'no':

Either you're carefree and untroubled by the domestic travails of modern life, or you're basically a bit of a numpty.

FAMILIES AT WAR

'As one grows older, one becomes wiser and more foolish.'

FRANÇOIS, DUC DE LA ROCHEFOUCAULD

Most family arguments are ignited by seemingly trivial matters and are a product of human beings living together in close quarters. When you're growing up, especially during your teenage years, these little gripes and moans seem designed simply as a way for your parents to get at you. It's irksome then when you find the same petty irritants that used to wind up your parents now shredding your own fragile nerves. Be it losing the TV remote control down the back of the sofa or leaving the milk out of the fridge; not locking the back gate or hanging up the towels after a shower. Little by little those things your parents used to moan about have somehow finally got to you too. The following list cites some of the most common gripes – do you recognize any from your own childhood?

Are You Turning Into Your Dad?

1. 'Who do you think is going to clean this up?'

2. 'Do you think I'm running a hotel here?'

3. 'Where have I put my keys? I had them two minutes ago!'

4. 'We're not watching this rubbish! Put the news on.'

5. 'Come on, you've been on that computer long enough – now it's someone else's turn.'

6. 'Is it really necessary for you to call your best friend every night? This phone bill's astronomical!'

7. 'Turn it down!'

8. 'Who last had the remote control?'

9. 'Will you hurry up brushing your teeth, I'm bursting for the toilet!'

10. 'Be back no later than 10 p.m. or else you're grounded.'

'Parents are not interested in justice. They are interested in peace and quiet.'

BILL COSBY

'Forty is the old age of youth; fifty is the youth of old age.'

FRENCH PROVERB

HORROR HOLIDAYS

PART ONE: A LITTLE JAUNT ABROAD

> 'I did not fully understand the dread term
> "terminal illness" until I saw Heathrow for
> myself.'
>
> DENNIS POTTER

Previous trips to foreign fields were quests for adventure and high living. That shameful lads' holiday still causes you to wake up sweating in the middle of the night, and the less said about the stag party to Vegas the better, but in the main you consider yourself reasonably well travelled and able to adapt to different cultures. Time to take the family on its first jaunt abroad? Think again. Somewhere in the dim and distant past your parents may have taken you on a package trip or camping holiday. Ask them what their abiding memories of these family occasions were and you'll likely find they're ones of being stressed out and largely disappointed with the whole venture. Ignore these pertinent observations and you'll be doomed to make the same mistakes …

Planning Makes Imperfect

List Mania

My father loves planning and as a child I was
required to make a pre-holiday checklist. Not
sharing my dad's penchant for list-making,
I'd scribble down a few things, avoiding any
specifics, and then shove some clothes into
a suitcase. The night before departure, Dad
would appear at my bedroom door and
insist on 'signing off' my list. At this point
he'd become exasperated at my haphazard
approach. 'Clothes!' he'd explode. 'What
clothes? Warm clothes? Summer clothes?
Beach clothes? Under clothes? How
many pairs of socks and pants have you
packed?' And I'd be forced to unpack and lay
everything out and count all the individual
items before putting them back in my case.

ROD, THIRTY-SEVEN

'The only way of catching a train I ever
discovered is to miss the train before.'

G.K. CHESTERTON

> 'When preparing to travel, lay out all your
> clothes and all your money. Then take half
> the clothes and twice the money.'
>
> SUSAN HELLER

The Early Bird Gets to Be First on the Plane

First in the Queue

Whenever we went on holidays abroad my dad
had an obsession with getting to the airport at
least three hours before take-off. We'd stand
around for ages waiting for the check-in desk
to open, and we were always the first in the
queue. Having checked in, Dad would then
drag us through into the departure lounge,
steadfastly refuse to let us go round the shops
or play on the arcade machines ('rip-off – save
your money for your holiday') and make us
wait at the departure gate. Often we were
there so early our flight hadn't come up on the
information boards and we'd just stand there
staring at the screen, waiting for it to appear ... I
used to pray our flight wouldn't be delayed.

JANE, THIRTY-FIVE

When In Rome ...

Franglais

My father had this embarrassing habit on holidays abroad of trying to 'fit in' with the locals. This usually manifested itself through enthusiastically practising his negligible French skills whenever possible. Most of the time in French resorts people would reply in English, but this wouldn't stop him – he'd soldier on to that excruciating point where whomever he was talking to would start to suspect he was taking the piss out of them and would scowl and walk away. On the occasions when they replied in French he'd get completely confused, get out his 1950s English/French phrase book, flick frantically through the pages and then point triumphantly at what he wanted to say.

GAVIN, FORTY-TWO

'I dislike feeling at home when I am abroad.'
GEORGE BERNARD SHAW

> 'I don't hold with *abroad*. I think foreigners
> speak English when our backs are turned.'
>
> QUENTIN CRISP

Just Like Mama Used to Make

My dad doesn't really have particularly catholic
tastes when it comes to food and drink – I'd say
he's very much a meat-and-two-veg type of
bloke. For some reason this would completely
change when we went abroad. He would read
up beforehand what the local speciality was
and would insist on trying it out. 'When in Rome,
when in Rome,' he would say, as he struggled
manfully with a plate of boiled ox tongue in a
local cafe he'd had recommended to him by
the barman at the hotel. The dish was always
delicious, of course, and any subsequent stomach
upset Dad suffered was never blamed on it,
despite my mother's protests to the contrary.

SUE, FORTY-EIGHT

> 'Like our shadows,
> Our wishes lengthen as our sun declines.'
>
> EDWARD YOUNG, 'NIGHT-THOUGHTS'

Le Plat de Jour

SOMETIMES THE BULL WINS...

An Englishman touring Spain stopped at a local restaurant following a day of sightseeing. While sipping his sangria, he noticed a sizzling, scrumptious-looking platter being served at the next table. Not only did it look good, the smell was wonderful. He asked the waiter, 'What is that you just served?'

The waiter replied, 'Ah, *señor*, you have excellent taste! Those are bulls' testicles from the bullfight this morning. A delicacy!'

The Englishman, though momentarily daunted, said, 'What the hell, I'm on vacation! Bring me an order!'

The waiter replied, 'I'm so sorry, *señor*. There is only one serving per day because there is only one bullfight each morning. If you come early tomorrow and place your order, we will be sure to save you this delicacy!'

The next morning, the Englishman returned, placed his order, and then that evening he was served the one and only special delicacy of the day. After a few bites he called to the waiter and said, 'These are delicious, but they are much, much smaller than the ones I saw you serve yesterday!'

The waiter shrugged his shoulders and replied, '*Si, señor*. Sometimes the bull wins.'

Don't Do as Dad Did

Why Go All-Inclusive ...

I realized only recently that I might be turning into my dad when I very nearly bought a second-hand camper van. My parents had one when I was a kid and I've fond memories of it. I mentioned to my mum about my prospective purchase, thinking she'd approve, but was taken aback when she begged me not to. 'That damn thing was the bane of my life,' she said. 'It very nearly caused a divorce.' My mum then went into a diatribe about the number of ill-starred holidays the camper was involved in and the two occasions when the van broke down and we had to be towed back to the ferry port in France.

It seems the main problem was that the camper van was barely roadworthy when my dad bought it, but he had the idea he could fix it up. Apparently he would spend every weekend for months 'fiddling about with it' in preparation for the family camping holiday to France and would convince my mum it was 'purring like a baby'. We'd set off on holiday and would barely get across the Channel before the baby would start screaming and the van would break down, causing us to abandon our trip. I asked my mum what Dad would have said about my plans to buy a van (he died five years ago). 'Oh he'd have said go for it, but would then drive you mad by coming round every weekend to poke his nose under the bonnet to tinker with it.'

KEITH, FIFTY-ONE

'The time to enjoy a European trip is about three weeks after unpacking.'

GEORGE ADE, *FORTY MODERN FABLES*

'Travel is fatal to prejudice, bigotry, and narrow-mindedness, and many of our people need it sorely on these accounts. Broad, wholesome, charitable views of men and things cannot be acquired by vegetating in one little corner of the earth all one's lifetime.'

MARK TWAIN

Speak Slowly

Two English tourists are on a cycling holiday in Wales when they stop for lunch in the town of Llanfairpwllgwyngyllrobwlllllantysiliogogogoch on Anglesey. When the waitress brings them their food one of the tourists asks her a question.

'Excuse me, miss, could you settle an argument? Where exactly are we? And please speak very slowly so we can understand you properly.'

'Burr Gurr Kingg,' replies the girl.

You Know You're Turning into Your Dad on Holiday Abroad When ...

- You purchase a bespoke poolside outfit of designer swimming shorts, Hawaiian shirt and flip flops. You think there's a whiff of Sean Connery's Bond about your attire only for your teenage son to laugh uproariously when he first sees you.

- You spend hours shopping around for the best exchange rate and download a currency converter to your smartphone so you can irritate your partner by telling her how much everything she purchases would cost in England.

- On a trip to Italy you notice the ultra-stylish local middle-aged men carrying around their personal effects in little leather 'man bags'. Deciding it's a must-have accessory, you purchase one from a local market but on returning to England doubts start to creep in. After enduring quite a ribbing from your mates you go back to your trusty wallet. The man bag is then destined to be the last item left on the trestle table at car boot sales for evermore.

- Although not a natural linguist you convince yourself that your D in French is enough for you to get by. Your partner, however, is unconvinced and scolds you several times for speaking loudly and slowly and using the 'international language of gesture' too much.

- You buy at least three guidebooks for the place you're visiting and bore the rest of the family by pointing out any inconsistencies you find between them.

- You thoroughly humiliate your teenage kids by enthusiastically bellowing out Frank Sinatra songs at the hotel's karaoke night (something you wouldn't dream of doing at home).

- You flirt atrociously with the attractive divorcee holidaying alone at your hotel and invite her along on an excursion. You claim you feel sorry for her but your family accuse you of being a creepy old letch. In truth it's somewhere between the two camps, and sadly as near as you're going to get to a holiday romance for the rest of your life.

PART TWO: REDISCOVERING YOUR HOME COUNTRY

> 'A good traveller has no fixed plans, and is not intent on arriving.'
>
> LAO TZU (ANCIENT CHINESE PHILOSOPHER)

You get to a certain point in life when you're suddenly gripped by the nostalgia virus. The rose-tinted spectacles steam up as you recall the happy family holidays of your youth. Oh the larks you had during that week on the canal boat or the palace of unbridled fun that was the holiday camp on the seafront in the summer of eighty-two. Once the nostalgia virus has gripped, there's no turning back and it's time to rediscover what your own country has to offer by way of horror holidays.

Biting the Bullet

Money is tight, you're still paying off the previous year's all-inclusive holiday and you notice that a daily newspaper is offering family holidays to its readers for an unbelievably low price. You mention the offer to your partner, who is more than a little sceptical, pointing out that the apparent 'giveaway' price is because holiday parks are ghastly places that nobody in their right mind would ever visit. You say you've fond memories of trips to holiday camps when you were young, there'll be lots for the kids to do and if it really is that awful you can always come home. Reluctantly your partner agrees, but you can already tell her heart isn't in it.

Let Battle Commence

The first hurdle to negotiate before embarking on your bargain holiday adventure is the extraordinarily complex booking restrictions. Having spent weeks pinching the required number of tokens from the newspaper in your local greasy spoon, and diligently sticking them to the booking form, you then have to nominate five different destinations and holiday dates.

This provokes immediate ire from your partner,

who's rapidly having all her suspicions confirmed. Inevitably you get your fifth choice of holiday park, which you didn't particularly fancy visiting but had put down simply to satisfy the booking requirements. Luckily, you get the next school holiday so at least you don't have to take the kids out of lessons for the week.

Are We There Yet?

Finally the day arrives, you pack up the car with supplies of baked beans, crisps and gravy granules as your partner has decided that, because it's self-catering, you're going to do all the cooking and not spend a penny in any of, what the brochure describes as, the 'excellent on-site eateries with competitive prices'.

After taking a wrong turn en route and getting hopelessly lost, you finally get to the holiday park (which for some reason doesn't seem to be signposted from the nearest main road) and although not quite what you expected, the accommodation looks spacious, clean and modern. Feeling more or less vindicated, you bound into the reception feeling pretty pleased with yourself. It's from this point that the full horror of what you're about to submit your family to rears its ugly head.

Is This It?!

It seems the bargain price advertised in the daily paper refers only to the dubious privilege of staying in one of the on-site caravans; should you wish to use any of the caravan's facilities, i.e. wash, cook or sleep in a bed with sheets, additional costs are incurred. Likewise, should you wish to use the indoor swimming pool or even have a drink in the bar, a further surcharge in the form of a 'Family Fun Pass' is required to be paid in advance. Already the rot has set in.

The hatchet-faced woman on reception asks you if you'd like to upgrade your standard accommodation to deluxe. Having paid out almost double to make the basic accommodation remotely habitable, you're reluctant to shell out even more cash. It's at this point that you realize the sparkling white caravans you passed on the driveway aren't going to be the ones you'll be staying in. Instead you're given a site map directing you to your bargain-basement hovel at the back-end of the site.

Holiday Heaven?

After some navigation problems, you finally find your six-berth stationary caravan, only for your partner to immediately question the validity of the six-berth claim as there only seem to be two beds: one single and one double. You make the first of many disconsolate trudges back to reception to see if there's been a mistake with your booking.

It seems six-berth refers not to the number of beds but to the maximum number of people allowed to stay in the caravan according to health and safety restrictions. Hatchet Face on reception informs you that you can hire fold-up camp beds at an additional cost (sheets and blankets extra) or, if you prefer, you could upgrade to the deluxe accommodation. You hire two camp beds and are introduced to Dave the maintenance man – a swarthy chap who is almost unbearably jolly.

Dave loads the two camp beds into the trailer of his compact tractor and gestures for you to jump on. A white-knuckle ride across the site ensues as you hold on for dear life as Dave hares hell for leather, laughing maniacally at your visible discomfort. You begin to suspect that Dave is a psychopath.

Holiday Hell

With basic domestic arrangements for your stay seemingly sorted out, at least for the time being, you round up the family and venture into the entertainment complex to see what it has to offer. After running the gauntlet of amusement arcades and cynically situated gift shops you finally locate the 'Swim Plex', only to find that access is restricted at peak times of the day. Irritation mounting, you march back to confront Hatchet Face, who explains that if you want to use the pool at peak times then you need to upgrade to the deluxe Family Fun Pass. The hole in your wallet has irreparably deepened and your partner refuses to speak to you for the rest of your miserable stay.

Happy holidays!

EMBARRASSING YOUR OFFSPRING

DADS AND THEIR DAUGHTERS

'If you have never been hated by your child,
you have never been a parent.'

BETTE DAVIS

Dads delight in embarrassing their offspring. And there's nothing more excruciating than the first time you bring your new squeeze home to meet the parents. Will Mum mention that time you wet yourself in infants? Will Dad insist on telling his awful jokes just to fill the silences? Dad is never more embarrassing than when his daughter first brings home her errant, spotty-faced boyfriend – the knives are out and Dad'll do all he can to make sure the boy knows his place. Do you now find yourself puffing out your chest and flexing your biceps every time your own daughter dares to mention the 'b' word?

'A father is always making his baby into a little woman. And when she is a woman he turns her back again.'

ENID BAGNOLD

Dealing With Your Daughter's First Boyfriend

It's the day that all fathers dread: when your little girl comes home with her first boyfriend. Online parenting websites provide a variety of different perspectives on dealing with the situation, ranging from sitting the young man down and interrogating him, to browsing social networking sites and spying on his whereabouts.

The following scenarios might give you some idea of how best to act, but in truth one can only provide support and hope for the best as often the first boyfriend will be followed by the first heartbreak, and it's important Dad is there to pick up the pieces. Alternatively, you could take a leaf out of Hollywood actor Antonio Banderas' book – he cleans his shotgun when his daughter brings boyfriends home.

Starting Young

My daughter Aliza came home from school and, in a voice testing my reaction, announced she had a boyfriend. Aliza is five-and-a-half.

This isn't the first time Aliza has declared a special relationship with another child. But the language was new and more serious. When she was three, Aliza said that she was going to marry Ivan, a boy her junior and an important Jewish playmate. But Ivan's star faded because he slept with the light on. So Aliza realized that despite her friendship with Ivan, he was not a suitable mate.

Next came Nadav, a classmate from preschool who she now unfortunately doesn't get to see that often because they've since graduated to different kindergartens. But, alas, Nadav too had his faults – Aliza found out that Nadav eats meat. Now another has caught her eye.

These days Aliza is speaking about a boyfriend. Something about the word 'boyfriend' signals to me that Aliza's social landscape is evolving and so must my reactions. So I slipped into Jewish fatherly role and began, for the first time, to ask certain questions:

'Is he Jewish?'

'Yes.'

'Does he smoke?'

'Abba, kids don't smoke!'

'Is he a vegetarian?'

'Abba, sometimes he's a vegetarian. He threw out his turkey sandwich today. He always wants to be near me, and during nap time he sleeps on the mat next to mine.'

Of course I'm overreacting, since Aliza is still only in kindergarten. But one day she really will have a romantic relationship and her own means of transportation. So I should view the recent events as reminders that if I want Aliza to date a Jewish, non-smoking vegetarian, I should start reinforcing these values now while she's still my little girl.

YOUSEF ABRAMOWITZ, *JEWISH NEWS*

'Watching your daughter being collected by her date feels like handing over a million-dollar Stradivarius to a gorilla.'

JIM BISHOP

Cat Meat

I was recently talking to my daughter about when she was seventeen and the first time she brought home a guy to meet her mother and I. My daughter and her brother had tried to warn this guy about me, and he seemed somewhat shaken when he arrived. He came to pick her up to go to a party and, whilst I know my little angel and I trust her judgement, his definitely needed fine-tuning. I shook the young man's hand and asked him to have a seat. We exchanged pleasantries, and just sort of felt each other out. However, he was clearly nervous and piped up with, 'Don't worry, I'll take good care of her and bring her home on time.' To which I replied, 'Have a good time, but if you make my daughter cry I'll put you through a meat grinder and feed you to my cats.'

He just looked at me at first, then he looked at my daughter, and she looked him dead in the eye and said, 'He means it, don't piss him off.' She didn't smile, not even slightly – didn't even bat an eyelid. That's my girl! At this point I could see this poor boy chewing it over, and I knew the carpet had been pulled from underneath him. He had her back ten minutes early.

GREGORY, SIXTY-NINE

Get the Message

When I was about nineteen I was dating a girl whose father absolutely hated me. No matter what I did, or how hard I tried to please him, the guy just hated me even more. So after about a month of trying to make my life miserable, the guy learnt that I played guitar. Unbeknownst to me, her father was an official in the musicians' union and very influential in deciding who did and didn't work on Long Island. Her father then changed his whole attitude toward me and assumed the 'Good Cop' role and got me into the union. Within a week he had me playing virtually non-stop every weekend with various wedding bands. I was working every Friday night, all day Saturday and Saturday night, and all day Sunday, leaving little time for me to see his daughter. After a few months of this schedule, the daughter broke it off with me because I wasn't spending enough time with her. To top it all, one week after she broke up with me, the union called to say it had no more gigs for me. The dad's message came through loud and clear.

DAN, FORTY-THREE

Meet the Family

A friend of mine was concerned about his sixteen-year-old daughter's first boyfriend. He had met the boy a couple of times and had found him to be surly and unresponsive. The boy was two years older than his daughter and had dropped out of college and had no job prospects other than vague ambitions to be a musician. After a series of heated arguments with his daughter my friend was at his wits' end. He couldn't forbid his daughter from seeing the boy, as that would just cause his daughter, with whom he had always had a close relationship, to resent him.

On the other hand his daughter was clearly besotted with the boy and he noticed she'd started smoking and drinking alcohol, which he attributed to the influence of her boyfriend.

Finally he came up with an ingenious plan. He rang several of his friends and family and arranged for them to put together a series of social gatherings on consecutive weekends for about a month. He then invited along his daughter's boyfriend to all of the events. At each event, the boyfriend was sat down by different people and asked polite questions about his future plans and ambitions and on more than one occasion given a guitar and press-ganged into performing for the entertainment of the guests. Finally it paid off and the boyfriend broke off the relationship, largely so he didn't have to attend any more of the gatherings. The daughter was heartbroken but my friend was able to use the 'you were too good for him' line when comforting her.

SIMON, FIFTY-TWO

'Any astronomer can predict with absolute accuracy just where every star in the universe will be at eleven-thirty tonight. He can make no such prediction about his teenage daughter.'

JAMES T. ADAMS

'The father of a daughter is nothing but a high-class hostage. A father turns a stony face to his sons, berates them, shakes his antlers, paws the ground, snorts, runs them off into the underbrush, but when his daughter puts her arm over his shoulder and says, "Daddy, I need to ask you something," he is a pat of butter in a hot frying pan.'

GARRISON KEILLOR

The Sharp End

Whenever I took my latest boyfriend home to meet my parents my dad would insist on taking him into his study to show him his collection of ancient Samurai swords. Dad would take each sword out of its presentation case and explain in great detail where it came from and what it was used for. Then he'd go into one about the Samurai code of honour and how the swords were so sharp they could behead a dishonourable man with one swish. He just did it to intimidate them and a few certainly got a bit weirded out by it all.

REBECCA, THIRTY-SIX

'I have three daughters and I find as a result I played King Lear almost without rehearsal.'

PETER USTINOV

Extreme Parenting

The award for the most extreme response of a dad to his daughter's inappropriate boyfriend surely goes to German Helmut Seifert. Seifert learned via an anonymous phone call that his seventeen-year-old daughter was involved in a relationship with a man named Philip Genscher, who was forty years her senior. Seifert petitioned the local police to intervene in the relationship but was told it was not a police matter and, as Seifert's daughter was above the age of consent, there wasn't anything they could do about it. Incensed by the police's attitude and his daughter's refusal to break off the relationship, Seifert decided to take matters, quite literally, into his own hands.

After enlisting the help of two work colleagues, Seifert went to Genscher's house, ordered him to remove his trousers and castrated his testicles with a bread knife.

Seifert was subsequently arrested for attempted murder but remained unrepentant for his actions telling police, 'I saw it as my duty as a father.'

'Many a man wishes he were strong enough to tear a telephone book in half – especially if he has a teenage daughter.'

GUY LOMBARD

'Sometimes the poorest man leaves his children the richest inheritance.'

RUTH E. RENKEL

DADS BEHAVING BADLY

> 'Every man over forty is a scoundrel.'
> GEORGE BERNARD SHAW,
> *MAXIMS FOR REVOLUTIONISTS*

From embarrassing your kids, to bragging about your own past exploits, the beauty of old age means you just don't give a fig about what people think of you. As you approach middle age, bask in the glory that mischief is now yours for the making!

Funny Guy

My dad used to delight in embarrassing me in front of my friends. He would always open the front door and invite them into the kitchen for a coffee. He'd then make these stupid jokes and start showing off. All of my friends thought he was really funny and used to say how they wished their dads were like him. I used to shrivel with embarrassment and try and usher them upstairs to my room to stop him flirting with them all.

JANE, THIRTY-NINE

Stop it, Dad!

My dad's in his nineties and has become obsessed with talking about his sexual exploits. I was never really aware when I was growing up just what a love rat he'd been. He was away from home quite a lot but his job entailed a lot of travelling so we always assumed he was off on a business trip. He used to bring back presents for my sisters and I, so we were always excited to see him home again.

But it turns out he had a girl in every town, so to speak. I assume my mum knew about most of them, or turned a blind eye in order to protect us. The problem now is that whenever there's a family get-together my dad invariably has a few too many and starts loudly discussing his 'Casanova Years', as he likes to call them, regaling us with tales of the 'extraordinary' décolletage of Betsy, or some other woman he picked up on a train (whose name he can't remember). My mum just rolls her eyes and gives him a 'yes, dear' look. The rest of the family is left squirming in their seats.

The strange thing is he tells the stories so vividly they sound totally plausible, but my eldest sister maintains he just likes embarrassing us all with his warped fantasies. I guess we will never know the truth.

TONY, SIXTY-ONE

Calm Down!

My dad was always a very placid and patient man and hardly ever used to raise his voice. But just lately he seems prone to losing his rag. Just the other day he nearly got into a fight in a restaurant when the mobile phone belonging to another diner went off very loudly. The diner then proceeded to have a long and very audible conversation for over five minutes. I could see that my dad was getting very agitated but I wasn't prepared for what came next.

When the diner had finished his call my dad walked over to his table. 'Give me your phone,' he barked. The loud diner was so startled he handed my dad his phone, maybe thinking he needed to make an urgent call. My dad promptly dropped the man's phone into the water jug and walked away!

JIM, FORTY-FIVE

'Old people do more scandalous things than any rebel you care to name. It's because they don't give a damn, they couldn't give a rat's arse what you think. If they're over eighty years old they are leaving soon so why should they care?'

CHRIS ISAAK

'I'm a different guy here in my sixties, I don't have the same libido. It used to be that I didn't think I could sleep if I wasn't involved in some kind of amorous contact. Well, I spend a lot of time sleeping alone these days.'

JACK NICHOLSON

TRANSPORT

DRIVING: THE CAR'S THE STAR (OR IS IT?)

> 'Be wise with speed;
> A fool at forty is a fool indeed.'
>
> EDWARD YOUNG

The sudden urge to purchase a sporty car is one of the clichés of a midlife crisis. As if a new zippy automobile can somehow make up for all the deficiencies that the onset of middle age brings. However, there are different types of dad driver and not all of them are born-again boy racers. Interestingly, recent research by the RAC revealed that men aged between forty-five and sixty are twice as likely to drink and drive as younger men between seventeen and twenty-four. Clearly the message about the perils of drink-driving has got through to the younger generation, whilst their older counterparts seem to think it still acceptable.

The Perils of Middle-Aged Drivers

Steaming In

I walked halfway into a conversation some colleagues were having about convertible cars. Deadly mistake – I was passing comment without knowing what was going on. I launched into a tirade about balding middle-aged men in soft tops, just like my dad used to when I was little, and found I was challenged quite strongly by a balding middle-aged bloke I thought I knew very well. I found his tirade odd as this guy doesn't have a soft top but a normal saloon. Or so I thought. The next week I saw his brand-new convertible in the car park. He'd obviously had it on order and they must've been chatting about it before I steamed in and said my piece.

STEVE, THIRTY-EIGHT

Sunday Driver

I always thought my dad was a sensible driver but as he got older I started to fear for my safety. He suddenly became obsessed with petrol prices and would keep a notebook of the number of miles to the gallon he was doing each week. As a result, he started driving everywhere at a steady thirty miles an hour – classic Sunday driver – to try and save on petrol. It used to be so embarrassing on family outings with a long tailback following us around and angry drivers tailgating us for miles.

Recently I was out with my wife and kids for the day and we drove out for a picnic at the beach. We had a lovely afternoon but as we were packing up the car to go home she took the keys off me. 'You're starting to drive like your dad and I want to get the kids in bed early tonight,' she said.

CRAIG, FORTY-EIGHT

Feeling Woozy

My father ran his own haulage firm, which he set up after the war. He used to drive all over Europe and drank on the job every day. He was still driving well into his seventies until he finally got caught. Amazingly, he got away with a caution, despite being well over the limit, but he was completely unrepentant about it. I tried to explain to him that these days drinking and driving is totally unacceptable. But he wasn't having a word of it. He reckons drink-driving regulations don't take into account how long you've been driving around half-drunk and that a couple of beers doesn't affect him in the way it would teetotallers. This is certainly one way in which I *won't* be turning into my dad.

RAY, FIFTY-THREE

Daredevil Dad

My dad had a proper ritual when driving. He would make sure everyone had their seat belts on before setting off. Once we were all strapped in he would put on his 'driving gloves' and his flat cap and turn and say, 'Hold on to your hats!' We would then trundle off at a very Sunday driver pace until we got to a dual carriageway, when he would say, 'Let's see how fast this baby can go,' and drive about five miles an hour faster.

JOHN, FIFTY-SEVEN

The Five Types of Dad on the Road

1. The Road Safety Freak

Obsessed with speed cameras and traffic calming systems, the road safety freak insists that all passengers 'buckle up' before he turns on the ignition. A proud member of the AA (although he has never had to call them out in thirty years), he drives everywhere at a steady thirty-five miles an hour apart from on the motorway, when he really lets his hair down and does a steady forty-five in the middle lane. The road safety freak can often be seen on Sunday mornings with his head under the bonnet, checking the water and oil and making a few 'minor adjustments', regardless of whether they're necessary or not.

Steady as He Goes

My dad seemed to transform into a middle-aged driver overnight. One minute he was haring down the motorway in the outside lane, Dire Straits blaring out of the stereo, the next he was pulling out gingerly from the slip road, the sound of frustrated horns following him wherever he drove. I hope it doesn't happen to me ...

BEN, FORTY-ONE

2. The Classic Car Owner

The Classic Car Owner scours the classified ads every week looking for a bargain. Typically he wants a Jensen Interceptor, and swoons at the thought of an Aston Martin, but has to make do with an old Ford, which he 'ironically' soups up with spoilers, polka-dot seat covers and fluffy dice. This 'project' costs him a fortune in time and money just to get the old rust bucket on the road and, when he's not scratching his head trying to work out what's gone wrong now, he's trawling the internet looking for parts and sharing his thoughts with other similarly anally retentive middle-aged men. Other cars they may own are just about anything that has an owners' club (e.g. old style Minis, 2CVs, MGs ...) that runs regular drivers' rallies.

3. The Born-Again Boy Racer

You know the type – thinning on top but still grows his hair long. The pony tail is a telltale sign, as is anyone over forty driving a softtop convertible. They are the Born-Again Boy Racer! All of their hopes and ambitions are encapsulated in that brand-spanking-new 'pussy magnet' (or so they think!) In truth they're a laughing stock to everybody who knows them and no amount of showing off about 'how fast it goes on an open stretch between nought to sixty' can convince. They're prone to racing people (usually over half their age) at traffic lights and playing Genesis at obnoxiously loud levels when they have the top down.

4. The Advanced Skills Driver

Nobody really liked their driving instructor. A weird breed of social inadequates and neo-Nazis who can't understand why most right-minded people see driving as a means to an end and not a vital cornerstone of civilization. The Advanced Skills Driver is a middle-aged man who's taken his advanced test and, as a result, believes he's achieved a higher state of consciousness. A devotee of *Top Gear* and Formula One, he's incapable of taking a short trip to his local supermarket without getting enraged at the un-road-worthiness of most other motorists. The archetypal backseat driver, he'll pick up on every little indiscretion on the rare occasions he isn't behind the wheel.

5. The Big is Beautiful Driver

Drivers of large petrol-guzzling people carriers and four-by-fours display particular piety when it comes to parking. The 'baby on board' bumper sticker could just as easily apply to the person behind the wheel as to their offspring. They can be observed in their natural habitat at weekends in the car park of the local retail outlet: driving round and round, indignant with rage that there aren't enough designated 'parent and infant' spaces, and so they park their thunderous tank of a vehicle across two spaces in puerile protest.

Testing Times

I recently took a minibus driving test for work. The instructor was one of those advanced skills drivers – absolutely insufferable. He kept banging on about 'reading the road' and developing 'powers of anticipation'. It was all a bit zen, but it's hard to get into the required meditative state when you're in control of a minibus on a busy dual carriageway.

JOHN, FORTY-ONE

You know you're a middle-aged driver when:

- You have a tin of hard-boiled sweets in the glove box.

- Your motto is 'we'll get there when we get there'.

- The thought of crumbs on the floor of your freshly vacuumed car brings you out in a cold sweat.

- You have an encyclopedic knowledge of most car types.

- It takes you a good hour to prepare yourself for a five-minute journey.

Pipped to the Post

My dad was very proud of his 4x4 but
he never learned how to manoeuvre it. I
remember one time he'd spent ages scoping
out a very busy supermarket car park in order
to find the optimum space – close to the exit
and far away from the trolley park – only
to then spend an age getting himself into
position to reverse in. He was so slow going
about it this lady in a mini drove straight into
the space before my dad even got a look in.
I've never seen him look so angry! I, on the
other hand, couldn't stop laughing …

GRAHAM, THIRTY-SEVEN

'If one is not going to take the necessary
precautions to avoid having parents, one
must undertake to bring them up.'

QUENTIN CRISP, THE NAKED CIVIL SERVANT

Cycling: MAMIL – Middle-Aged Men in Lycra

'Nobody grows old merely by living a number of years. We grow old by deserting our ideals. Years may wrinkle the skin, but to give up enthusiasm wrinkles the soul.'

SAMUEL ULLMAN

Recent research has shown a sudden rise in the number of middle-aged men taking up cycling as a hobby or sport. As a result a new acronym has come into the common lexicon – the MAMIL: Middle-Aged Men in Lycra.

Midlife Crisis

Several media commentators have suggested that the purchase of expensive, carbon fibre road bikes has replaced the convertible sports car as the totem of a middle-aged man lurching towards a midlife crisis. The fact that they then feel the need to literally pour themselves into gaudily coloured, obscenely tight-fitting lycra cycling shorts adds to the notion that they're a walking (or, in this case, cycling) anachronism.

If you glance around any municipal park or popular cycle path of a summer weekend you'll notice hordes of MAMILs, red-faced and puffing around on their bikes, stopping to check their section times and to swig from their sports water bottles before manfully soldiering on.

Perhaps this isn't such a bad thing. The health benefits of regular exercise are well documented and there's always something to be said for getting out in the fresh air.

Cycling also has the advantage of being easy to do. Everyone had a bike when they were young and, once you've mastered the basics, it's a skill you never forget. As a form of exercise it's easy to pick up at a later stage in life and has advantages over, say, joining a gym, because you don't need to feel intimidated about the state of your figure or embarrassed about your lack of fitness.

The Classic Signs

The classic MAMIL dad can often be seen with his children in tow too, either in the form of a special attachment to his own bike, or dutifully following behind like baby ducks on a pond. A middle manager with environmental concerns (cycling is, by definition, very green), the MAMIL shows an admirable lack of concern for his appearance. The lycra shorts are surely a fashion faux pas but they've become so much part of the uniform that nobody will bat an eyelid when you race across the park on a sunny Sunday morning.

Accessorize

As with anything that comes under the heading 'symptoms of a midlife crisis', cycling provides opportunities for accessorizing. Like golf, companies wishing to exploit the cycling bug have been quick to bring out a range of hi-tech gadgets and gismos, none of which are strictly necessary, but are cool nonetheless. These include thoroughly superfluous items such as cameras that attach to your cycling helmet and MP3 players you connect to the bike to safely listen to music without headphones. Far cooler and more useful are miniature all-in-one tool kits, like a Swiss Army knife specially designed for all things bike related, and some extraordinarily expensive lightweight, high-pressure tyre pumps.

You Know You're a MAMIL If ...

- You see nothing wrong with discussing the connection between hydration and urine.

- You find your Shimano touring shoes to be more comfortable and stylish than your new trainers.

- You refuse to buy a settee because that patch of wall space is taken up by the bike.

- You have more money invested in your bike clothes than in the rest of your combined wardrobe.

- Biker chick means black lycra, not leather, and a Marinoni, not a Harley.

- Your bike is worth more than your car.

Are You Turning Into Your Dad?

- You view crashes as an opportunity to upgrade components.

- You clean your bike(s) more often than your house.

- You empathize with the roadkill.

- A measurement of 44-36-40 doesn't refer to the latest Playboy centrefold, but that new gear ratio you were considering.

- You wear your heart monitor to bed to make sure you stay within your target zone during any extracurricular activities.

- You experience an unreasonable envy over someone who has bar end extenders longer than yours.

- Despite all that winter weight you put on, you'll take off weight by buying titanium components.

- There's no time like the present for postponing what you ought to be doing and go cycling instead ...

A MAMIL Joke to Tell Cycling Mates Over a Beer

Two pieces of black tarmac are standing chatting at the bar, when in walks a piece of green tarmac.

The piece of green tarmac demands a pint of bitter from the landlord in a menacing manner, downs it in one, slams his money on the bar and walks out.

The landlord turns to the two pieces of black tarmac and says, 'Well, I'm glad he didn't cause any trouble – I've heard he's a bit of a cycle path.'

LEGACY

Too Much to Live Up To?

> 'He wants to live on through something – and in his case, his masterpiece is his son. All of us want that, and it gets more poignant as we get more anonymous in this world.'
>
> ARTHUR MILLER

Those of us who worry that we might be turning into our dads should spare a thought for the offspring of high-achieving parents. Often the pressure that they will follow in their father's footsteps has proved beyond some born from a gene pool of natural talent. When former tennis champion Steffi Graf gave birth to the son of fellow ace Andre Agassi, Ladbrokes would only offer odds of ten to one that the child would one day win Wimbledon. Not too much to live up to then?

The following list of fathers and sons shows how the weight of expectation can hang heavy round the necks of some famous people's offspring.

I. Evelyn Waugh/Auberon Waugh

The Waughs were one of the most prominent literary dynasties. Evelyn's father and Auberon's grandfather was the prominent writer, critic and publisher Arthur Waugh. In this respect Auberon had more than just the considerable achievements of his famous father to look up to. Although a successful journalist in his own right, a quick comparison of Auberon's and Evelyn's relative careers puts the former very much in the shade:

- Evelyn Waugh served in the Second World War with the Royal Marines and received several medals and commendations for his bravery. Auberon Waugh did National Service in Cyprus but was decommissioned after accidentally shooting himself with a faulty machine gun.

- Evelyn Waugh's fifteen full-length novels are amongst the most revered in the canon of twentieth-century literature and have been made into many films and successful TV series, including *Brideshead Revisited*, *Vile Bodies* and *A Handful of Dust*. Auberon Waugh wrote five moderate novels, the most successful of which was the first, *The Foxglove Saga*, which he wrote whilst recovering in Italy after the accidental shooting incident.

- According to Graham Greene, Evelyn Waugh was 'the greatest novelist of my generation'. On the death of Auberon Waugh from a heart attack aged sixty-one, Polly Toynbee wrote him a damning obituary under the heading 'Ghastly Man'.

2. Robert Mitchum/James and Christopher Mitchum

Hollywood acting legend Robert Mitchum's two sons, James and Christopher, both trod the same career path as their father but didn't quite reach his legendary status. The eldest son, James, made his first screen appearance in 1949 but the highlight of his career didn't come until 1958, and even then it was only with a supporting role alongside his father in the cult crime drama *Thunder Road* (for which Mitchum senior also co-produced and co-wrote the screenplay). But James was unable to build upon this brief success and his career trundled along, ending with the big-budget epic *Gengis Khan* (1992) in which he starred alongside Charlton Heston. Hopes of a final hoorah were dashed, however, when the film ran out of money during shooting and was left unfinished.

Christopher Mitchum had marginally more success in his early career, after being taken under the wing of another legend, John Wayne. He cast Christopher in several of his late films, including *Chisum* and *Big Jake*. However, much like his brother, Christopher struggled to step out of his father's shadow and was consigned to supporting roles in low-budget TV movies.

'A photograph never grows old. You and I change, people change all through the months and years, but a photograph always remains the same. How nice to look at a photograph of mother or father taken many years ago. You see them as you remember them. But as people live on, they change completely. That is why I think a photograph can be kind.'

ALBERT EINSTEIN

3. Lawrence Peter 'Yogi' Berra/Dale Berra

Baseball Hall of Famer Lawrence Peter 'Yogi' Berra is widely considered to be the greatest catcher of all time. His list of achievements as both a player and manager range from thirteen World Series championships and three Major League Baseball MVP awards (Most Valuable Player) to being the only manager in baseball history to lead teams from both the American and National leagues to separate World Series. When Yogi hung up his gloves in 1965, the New York Yankees retired the number eight shirt in his honour. Now that's something to live up to.

Sadly the professional career of his son, Dale, failed to match that of his esteemed father. Dale's career started promisingly at the Pittsburgh Pirates, where he was a member of the 1979 World Series winning roster. However, beset by injuries and loss of form, Dale was released by Pittsburgh in 1984. The following year he joined his father at the Yankees, where Yogi was manager, but was almost immediately suspended for a season for taking cocaine. Dale's career never really got back on track after the drugs suspension and, after a brief stint with the Houston Astros (again under the stewardship of his father), Dale retired from baseball in 1988 aged thirty.

4. Ian Botham/Liam Botham

Being the son of one of English cricket's greatest ever players was a tall order from the outset and not helped by having a similar-sounding Christian name. Tabloid newspapers eager for any Botham-related trivia published photographs of Liam as a toddler with a cricket bat in his hand. 'He's a cheeky little bugger who thinks he's going to be better than his old man,' said his doting father at the time. However, credit should be given to Liam for giving it a go, and when he took five wickets on his first-class debut for Hampshire the press heralded a new saviour of English cricket. Perhaps wisely, Liam decided that the pressure to emulate the often superhuman feats of his father on the cricket field were a touch unfair and he took up rugby instead. Liam had a reasonably successful career as a professional rugby player before

'I grew up to have my father's looks, my father's speech patterns, my father's posture, my father's walk, my father's opinions and my mother's contempt for my father.'

JULES FEIFFER

> 'One night a father overheard his son pray,
> "Dear God, make me the kind of man my
> daddy is." Later that night, the father prayed,
> "Dear God, make me the kind of man my son
> wants me to be."'
>
> ANONYMOUS

> 'If you must hold yourself up to your children
> as an object lesson, hold yourself up as a
> warning not an example.'
>
> GEORGE BERNARD SHAW

injury caused him to retire at the age of twenty-seven.
Whilst Liam was not quite up to the sporting marks set
by his father, at least he didn't inherit any of Botham
senior's more boorish traits: trashing hotel rooms,
assaulting police officers and appearing in celebrity
pantomimes.

5. George Best/Calum Best

It's indisputable that George Best was a supremely gifted soccer player, particularly in his early heydays at Manchester United, where he was crowned European Footballer of The Year in 1968. George's off-field antics during the swinging sixties and seventies made him an icon as much as anything he achieved on the field. And in his native Belfast he's been immortalized in folklore with the saying 'Maradona good, Pele better, George BEST!'

Calum Best, George's only legitimately born offspring, might have inherited his father's penchant for glamour girls, but certainly hasn't been blessed with his football skills (or if he has, he certainly hasn't attempted to use them). A regular on 'celebrity' reality TV shows, apart from a very brief career as a fashion model, the fact that his surname happens to be Best remains just about the only significant thing about him.

'A man knows he is growing old because he begins to look like his father.'

GABRIEL GARCIA MARQUEZ,
LOVE IN THE TIME OF CHOLERA

FOLLOWING IN HIS FOOTSTEPS

Not all sons of famous fathers turn out to be quite so mediocre. The following crop of fathers and their equally successful – if not overachieving – sons, might convince you there's hope yet ...

I. Lord Randolph Churchill/Winston Churchill

Lord Randolph Churchill was a significant Victorian politician who held a number of key posts in Parliament, including Leader of The House of Commons. His eldest son, Winston, followed him into politics with the express intention of achieving high office and in so doing don 'his father's cape'. Sir Winston Churchill would certainly have made his father proud had Lord Randolph not died of syphilis when Winston was twenty-one years old. As Noel Coward memorably put it, 'he (Randolph Churchill) is utterly unspoiled by failure.'

2. Graham Hill/Damon Hill

There must be something in the genes of motor racing families as there have been several notable father/son combinations (the Andrettis, the Fittipaldis and the Villeneuves, to name three). However, the only father and son to both be crowned Formula One World Champion are the late Graham Hill and his son, Damon.

Graham Hill is the only motor racing driver to have won the triple crown of the Indy 500, Le Mans *and* the Monaco Grand Prix and was twice F1 Champion. But Damon's achievements are arguably the more considerable given that he was driving in an era far more hi-tech and cut-throat than his father's. Promoted from test driver with the Williams team to number one driver after the death of Ayrton Senna, Damon (who'd previously had an undistinguished career at the lower level of Formula 3000) really rose to the occasion. Hill was extremely unlucky not to win the world title in 1994, losing out by a single point after a controversial crash in the final race of the season, but made amends two years later. In four seasons driving for Williams, Damon Hill never finished lower than third in the drivers' championship and amassed twenty-one wins in sixty-four races. Graham would have been proud.

3. Tim Buckley/Jeff Buckley

Both father and son were prodigiously talented singer-songwriters and both died young at twenty-eight and thirty respectively. Jeff Buckley had little contact with his father during his formative years and when he embarked upon his career he was careful to distance himself from comparisons with his father's music. Although Tim Buckley released nine studio albums, some to high critical acclaim, commercial success largely eluded him. Jeff Buckley released just one album, *Grace*, and was working on a second when he accidentally drowned in 1997. But he's had considerable success since his untimely death, with his most famous song, a haunting cover of Leonard Cohen's 'Hallelujah', reaching number one in the US Billboard Digital Chart and number two in the UK singles chart in 2008. So, if you don't quite reach the dizzy heights you thought you might within your own lifetime, there's always the possibility of posthumous success.

'No matter how calmly you try to referee, parenting will eventually produce bizarre behaviour, and I'm not talking about the kids. Their behaviour is always normal.'

BILL COSBY

---

4. Rance Howard/Ron Howard

Rance Howard has appeared in over a hundred feature films and made numerous appearances on American television. The father of successful child actor Ron Howard (aka Ritchie Cunningham from *Happy Days*), Rance indulged his son's ambitions to direct feature films by persuading legendary B-movie producer Roger Corman to fund a script that he'd co-written with his son. The result was *Grand Theft Auto*, a screwball comedy that gave Corman a significant return on his investment by taking over fifteen million dollars at the US box office (the film was made for just over half a million).

The film proved to be a springboard for Ron Howard's career, and he's since gone on to direct many successful Hollywood feature films including *Apollo 13* and *A Beautiful Mind* (for which he received the Oscar for Best Director). Who'd have thought Ritchie Cunningham would turn out to be such a winner!

> 'What's all this fuss about fathers being present at the birth of their children? The way events are shaping, they'll be lucky to be present at the conception.'
>
> GEORGE H. DAVIES

5. Archibald Manning/Peyton Manning/Eli Manning

Archie Manning was a competent quarterback with the New Orleans Saints in the 1970s – good enough to be twice selected for the Pro Bowl, but hardly with a cabinet full of medals and trophies. No doubt Archie is proud of his professional career, but prouder still of the exploits of his sons Peyton and Eli. Peyton has led the unfashionable Indianapolis Colts to two Super Bowls and was voted Player of the Decade in 2009. Not to be outdone, younger brother Eli Manning, quarterback for the New York Giants, won the family's second Super Bowl ring in 2008. Imagine what family gatherings with those guys were like …

> 'Henry James once defined life as that predicament which precedes death, and certainly nobody owes you a debt of honour or gratitude for getting him into that predicament. But a child does owe his father a debt, if Dad, having gotten him into this peck of trouble, takes off his coat and buckles down to the job of showing his son how best to crash through it.'
>
> CLARENCE BUDINGTON KELLAND

TOP FIVE FATHER/SON RELATED SONGS

> 'If youth but knew; if age but could.'
>
> HENRI ESTIENNE

What better way to immortalize your love for your father than through the medium of song. From Phil Collins to Will Smith, the world of music is littered with doting odes from fathers to their sons and sons to their fathers … not to mention a novelty tune about a gun-toting son exacting revenge on his dad for giving him a girl's name.

> 'The kind of man who thinks that helping with the dishes is beneath him will also think that helping with the baby is beneath him, and then he certainly is not going to be a very successful father.'
>
> ELEANOR ROOSEVELT

1. 'Father to Son' – Phil Collins

Taken from 1989's …*But Seriously* solo album, 'Father to Son' has the former Genesis drummer giving some not particularly sage-like advice to his son about his love life.

Collins finishes his song with the reassuring refrain, 'I will be there.' In real life, however, Collins' expertise as a guru of love has been found somewhat wanting given that he has been married and acrimoniously divorced on three occasions.

2. 'A Boy Named Sue' – Johnny Cash

A novelty song which first appeared on Cash's legendary *Live At San Quentin* album, 'A Boy Named Sue' concerns the resentment felt by a son saddled with a girl's name by an errant father he's never met. When he finally meets his father he sets about exacting his revenge, only for his father to explain he gave him a girl's name to toughen him up. The son accepts his father's reasoning but still vows not to do the same to his own son.

3. 'A Song For Dad' – Keith Urban

New Zealand-born country rocker Keith Urban penned this tribute to his father for his breakthrough second album *Golden Road*. The song starts with Keith Urban noticing how much like his father he's become and he discusses his previous perception of his father as being overbearing and harsh, but comes to the realization that most of us eventually come to – everything your dad's done for you he's done out of love.

> 'Growing up my father used to say I could be whomever I wanted to be. What a cruel hoax that was! I'm still his son.'
>
> KENNY SMITH

4. 'Just the Two of Us' – Will Smith

Hollywood star Will Smith included this cover of Bill Withers' love song standard on his debut album – the modestly named, *Big Willie Style*. The accompanying video featured Smith's son Trey, thereby signalling that Smith had dedicated the song to his son.

5. 'Father and Son' – Cat Stevens

Cat Stevens showcased his extraordinary vocal talent with 'Father and Son' – his hypothetical conversation between a headstrong son and his cautionary father – adopting a high key for the son and a lower key for the father. In an exchange that's been played out in countless households of teenagers about to fly the nest, the father offers some much needed advice.

Sherman made the terrible discovery that men make about their fathers sooner or later ... that the man before him was not an aging father but a boy, a boy much like himself, a boy who grew up and had a child of his own and, as best he could, out of a sense of duty and, perhaps love, adopted a role called Being a Father so that his child would have something mythical and infinitely important: a Protector, who would keep a lid on all the chaotic and catastrophic possibilities of life.

TOM WOLFE, *THE BONFIRE OF THE VANITIES*

QUIZ: ARE YOU TURNING INTO YOUR DAD?

THE FINAL TEST

Section One: You Choose

The Simpsons or the news headlines?

The Wire or *Diagnosis Murder* repeats?

Jersey Shore or a sofa snore?

The latest big sports event or your local bowls team's annual tournament?

A night on the tiles or an early night tucked up with the latest international bestseller?

Martial arts classes or pottery classes?

A round of shots or a round of golf?

The latest smartphone with all the trimmings or your trusty pay-as-you-go brick?

A wild week in Ibiza or a walking holiday in the countryside?

Burning Man or the local folk festival (day pass)?

Section Two: What Is Your First Thought?

1. You're walking home from work on a Friday night and a group of young women pass. They're obviously dressed up for a night out and you couldn't help noticing how scantily clad they were. Is your first thought:

a) Something lustful and dark that you immediately try and extinguish from your mind?

DEAR ME!.. SHE'LL CATCH HER DEATH...

b) You worry that they're going to be very cold and feel concerned about the pressure on young women to conform in front of their peers?

2. Although you're thinning on top you've noticed your hair is getting rather long at the back. In short, you could do with a haircut and a new trendy men's barbershop has just opened along the road. Is your first thought:

a) Pop in and ask for an appointment – they could have some ideas of how to restyle you on the approach to middle age?

b) Go to your usual barbers for the bog-standard short back and sides, or maybe ask your wife or partner to give you a quick trim?

The Carpet Police

I used to laugh at my dad when he asked people to take off their shoes in the house so they didn't get mud on the nice new carpet he'd had laid, but I now find myself doing it in my own house. My wife cringes with embarrassment every time I ask a guest to remove their shoes, but I just can't help myself! I'll be asking them not to drop crumbs on the floor next . . .

NEIL, THIRTY-NINE

3. It's after 9 p.m. and there's a knock at the door. Not being accustomed to visitors turning up unannounced, is your first thought:

a) It may be a long-lost cousin who's tracked you down, or a dear friend in a time of need?

b) Ignore it; you'd remember if it was a takeaway delivery because they'd said it would be thirty minutes and you've been checking your watch every two minutes since placing the order and, although it's unlikely to be a murderous psychopath, it's almost certainly somebody who wants money off you in some way, shape or form?

4. It's a significant wedding anniversary and you feel you should treat your long-suffering partner, so you ask her what she'd like to do. She says she'd like to go to the latest 'hot' restaurant that's opened up nearby, which just happens to be owned by a famous TV celebrity chef. Is your first thought:

a) That sounds like a grand idea. It'll be expensive but I'll max out the credit card and we'll have a night to remember?

b) I'm sure I saw a deal in the local paper for two for the price of one dinners if you collect all the tokens and book six weeks in advance?

5. It's the festive season and the in-laws ('out-laws!') are coming to stay. You've been asked for a list of possible presents that you might like in order to avoid a surfeit of socks and toiletries. Is your first thought:

a) There's nothing I really want or need, just having my extended family for company is a gift in itself?

b) I really can't think of anything that, realistically, those parsimonious penny pinchers are going to buy me, so it's pants and socks for me again this year?

Section Three: Quick-Fire Round

Do you own a pair of leather driving gloves?

☐ **Yes**　　　　　　　☐ **No**

Do you watch holiday programmes on TV thinking, well I've seen all the sights now so what's the point in spending an arm and a leg going there?

☐ **Yes**　　　　　　　☐ **No**

Do you occasionally get nostalgic for foul food products from your youth (e.g. tinned spam fritters or Fray Bentos steak pies) only to find them deeply unsatisfying?

☐ **Yes**　　　　　　　☐ **No**

Do you find that you over-elaborate jokes and forget the punchline, or drag out amusing anecdotes until the point where you can tell your audience's eyes have glassed over but you soldier on regardless?

☐ **Yes**   ☐ **No**

Do you feel that your best days are behind you and that if only you'd taken that 'path less travelled' then everything could have been so different?

☐ **Yes**   ☐ **No**

Scoring

In section one you should award yourself one point for choosing the first option and two points for the second, e.g. if you chose an early night tucked up with the latest international bestseller over a heavy night on the tiles you score two. In section two if you chose answer a) you score one point, if b) you score two. In section three (hold on to your hats!) if you chose 'yes' you score one point, if 'no' then two.

20–25 points:

Hmm, you probably aren't turning into your dad and there could be various reasons for this. For example, have you ever noticed how you look more like your uncle than your dad? Alternatively, perhaps you just aren't ready to embrace the 'third wave' just yet. A word of warning though, nobody wants to be carrying on pretending to be young too far past their sell-by date.

25–35 points:

It's certainly true that you've picked up a few tricks from the old man along the way, whether you intended to or not. Gradually you'll come to embrace all those foibles and follies that used to get right up your nose. Perhaps you're still holding out for hopes and dreams? Maybe you'll realize them? Maybe your dream is to be just like your dad?

35+ points:

Congratulations! You really are a chip off the old block! So much so you may as well have just been grown in a laboratory of some sinister cloning factory. Sorry, that's a bit harsh. There's nothing wrong with spoken radio, cardigans or ale. Likewise there's nothing wrong with hating your in-laws or hankering after processed meat products from the 1970s. What you need to do now, though, is search for your 'inner dad' and embrace everything your old man has taught you, unwittingly or otherwise.

AFTERWORD

PLACEMENT, NOT POWER

I was told not to personalize this book too much and to 'give it a universality'. 'It's not all about you,' said my wife (although she says that with awful regularity about almost anything). However, I feel it would be doing my own father a considerable injustice if I didn't talk about him and, by extension, myself.

Let it Be

An important truth that my dad has taught me is that you have to let your children make their own decisions – of course you can advise them and steer them towards what you think is right, but ultimately the choice is theirs, and theirs alone, to make.

Always Be There

My early memories of my dad are that he was always supportive in whatever I was doing. What I've grown to realize though is that when other kids' dads were cheering their sons on playing for the local football team, my dad was the only parent shouting the sort of negative abuse you might hear from the terraces against the home team's dodgy goalkeeper.

'What on earth were you thinking?' he once asked when I missed a penalty in a shoot-out in a six-a-side tournament semi-final. 'Placement, not power!'

Fortunately our keeper saved two penalties so my team got through to the final, but my rush of blood to the head was what annoyed him most.

Generally speaking, my dad is very gentle and extraordinarily kind and thoughtful ... except when it comes to games. I don't recommend playing him at scrabble or chess or bowls or ... anything, for that matter.

The Ultimate Question

Do I think I'm turning into my dad? Well, weirdly, I've noticed my dad turning into my granddad: strict timekeeping, an obsessive/compulsive attachment to routine (they both get very uppity if Sunday lunch is delayed beyond its starting time of 1 p.m.) and getting upset if the home team wins the toss and doesn't bat first.

I've also noticed that the things that used to enrage my dad are actually random accidents. When I was a kid, my dad would get irate if any member of the family broke anything, and as I've got older I've realized this is because of his scientific background. The language philosopher Ludwig Wittgenstein proposed the theory that it's impossible to argue logically against a counter position that's illogical. And as a physics professor, my dad can't accept the random or the inexplicable.

As a result, I've heard him argue against injustice, inequality and prejudice, all of which, thanks to him, I've learnt are illogical, nasty accidents, if you like. We don't always agree but I do think my moral sensibilities come from my dad regarding what I think is right and wrong. I just need to chill out a bit when my mother-in-law breaks things.

I don't think I'm turning into my dad – I've always seen much more of my sister in him than I've recognized in myself. That said, I still feel like I'm learning from him and every moment we spend together is precious in that respect. No matter how much your parents can infuriate you, if ultimately you love them and respect them, then I can't see why anyone of us should worry about turning into them.

JOSEPH PIERCY

BIBLIOGRAPHY

Books

Bentley, Nicholas and Esar, Evan
The Treasury of Humorous Quotations
(J.M. Dent 1951)

Jarski, Rosemarie
The Funniest Thing You Never Said
(Ebury 2007)

Klein, Shelley
The Book of Senior Moments
More Senior Moments
(Michael O'Mara 2006/2007)

Lloyd, John and Mitchinson, John
Advanced Banter: The QI Book of Quotations
(Faber and Faber 2008)

Tibballs, Geoff
The Mammoth Book of Insults (Robinson 2004)
The Mammoth Book of Quotes (Robinson 2007)

Vale, Allison and Rattle, Allison
Wrinklies' Wit and Wisdom Forever
(Prion 2006)

Websites

www.brainyquote.com

www.quotationspage.com

www.wisdomquotes.com

www.dad.info

www.dads-space.com

www.fathers.com

www.facebook.com

Newspapers

The *Daily Mail*

The Guardian

The Times

ACKNOWLEDGEMENTS

I would like to offer my eternal love and thanks to the following people for their help and support with this project. Mathew Clayton and Katie Duce and everybody at Michael O'Mara Books for their unswerving encouragement and support, Aubrey Smith for his fantastic drawings and inspirations. Polly and Joanna for putting up with my bouts of angst and self-indulgence but most of all my dad, Alan Piercy, without whom this, quite literally, would not have been possible.

JOSEPH PIERCY